George Wither

Exercises vpon the first Psalme

George Wither

Exercises vpon the first Psalme

ISBN/EAN: 9783744778350

Printed in Europe, USA, Canada, Australia, Japan

Cover: Foto ©Lupo / pixelio.de

More available books at **www.hansebooks.com**

EXERCISES

VPON THE

FIRST PSALME.

Both in Profe and Verfe.

BY

GEORGE WITHER.

PRINTED FOR THE SPENSER SOCIETY.

1882.

EXERCISES
VPON THE
First PSALME.

Both in Prose and Verse.

By GEO: WITHER,
Of the Societie of
Lincolnes Inne.

But, his delight is in the Law of the LORD. &c.
PSAL. I. verf. 2.

LONDON,
Printed by *Edw. Griffin,* for *Iohn Harrifon,*
and are to be fold at his fhop, in *Pater
Nofter* Row, at the figne of the
Golden *Vnicorne.* 1620.

TO
THE NOBLE
YOVNG GENTLE-MAN,
Sʳ. IOHN SMITH, Knight;
onely Sonne to the honourable
Knight, Sʳ. THOMAS SMITH,
Gouernour of the *East-India*
Company, &c. The Author
of these Exercises, *heartily
wisheth all true happi-
nesse whatsoeuer.*

SIR,

Vch hath beene the re-
spect, and many the
courtesies; which, I
haue receiued from your no-
ble Father. And the greatest re-quitall

The Epistle

quitall I can giue him; is, to make my selfe (as far as in mee lyeth) such a one, as that hee neede not repent, nor be ashamed of the respect hee hath showne mee: and that, if I should dye vnable to repay his kindnesses; he might yet, haue some cause, to think his fauors not altogether lost vpon mee. Nay rather, might reckon them among the good deedes he hath done) in regard I haue made vse of them, (not to follow my pleasures, but) to enable me in some good endeauours.

Of which, this little volume is a part; & knowing, I should well

Dedicatorie.

well witneffe my loue vnto him, whenfoeuer I gaue good teftimony of mine honeft affection towards you. Lo, as a pledge therof, I confecrate to your vfe, thefe *Exercifes*. And, with your name, deliuer them ouer to the world. That, when, and wherefoeuer they fhall be read; you may be remembred, both for a louer of thefe kinds of ftudies, & a Fauourer of his, who was defirous to bee honeftly employed. For, fuch haue you approued your felfe towards mee, both in your courteous familiarity : and by that free acceffe, which in my meditations, I haue alwayes had

The Epistle

had to your Library.

Accept then these papers; & let it not be tedious vnto you, sometime to read them ouer. For, though I may be thought fitter by many, to accompany you in the way of pleasures: then to present you with any sound precepts of morality, or Religion. Yet, I hope, you shall finde me an Instrument: readier to encourage you, in euery of those vertues, wherwith your education hath acquainted your youth: then to whisper ought, that may bring you in loue with those vanities; whereunto, ouer-many other of our Gentry, are so much enclinde.

Dedicatorie.

clinde. For, though that way, I might haue more bettered my fortunes, and esteeme, among some men. This way, I am sure, I shall better satisfie my conscience, and my dutie to God.

Neuerthelesse, I prefer not this to instruct you; but, to be a Remembrancer, of those things, in which you haue alreadie beene instructed. For, your good Father, hath not onely largely prouided for you, the temporall felicities: but, asmuch, as in him lieth, prepared you for that *Blessednes*, which is treated of in these *Exercises*. More he cannot do; seeing,

The Epistle, &c.

seeing, it must be euerie mans particular endeauor, that shall purchase him this treasure, being the most invaluable that can be For, the greatest *Monarch* of the world, háth neither power to giue, nor take it, from you. Yea, and without it, the more of other blessings you possesse, the more miserable they will make you. But, I know, you will bee happie in the prosecution therof, that you may treble that happines, in the possession of it. And, to that end, you haue my prayers, who am

most faithfully yours,

G. W.

To the Reader.

*Know, that many of you, e're this time, expected the first Decade of the* Psalmes, *according to the promise, in my* Preparation. *And therfore, when you behold here, but a tenth part of it, I shall be thought to come too much short of what I intended. As indeed I doe (seeing, I then wanted not much, of hauing finished the whole* Decade *in that manner, as I purposed to set it forth) But, if it were here fitting (or any way for your profit) to discouer them, I might*

To the Reader.

I might giue vndenyable reasons (to excuse my selfe) which I now conceale.

Onely thus much, I will say. Few men consider, how many painefull dayes (after the maine labour is ended) the writing ouer againe of such a volume will aske; how many moneths it may be afterwards attended at the Presse; *how much charge, the Authors little means, may (without any profit of his labours) bee put to ; nor, through how many vnlooked-for troubles and businesses, hee must make way vnto the performance of it. For, if they did know, and weigh this ; so many, that are idle ones themselues, would not so often (as I heare they doe) blame my idlenesse.*

To the Reader.

idleneſſe. But, rather wonder, how; and when, I got meanes and time, to performe what is already done.

Diſcouragements, and hinderances, I haue had many, ſince I began to meddle with the Pſalmes. *But helps, or encouragements, I haue had none; no, not the leaſt part of one: ſaue the comforts, which I haue found, within mine owne heart. And they are ſo great, that I am ſtill reſolued to proceed in this work, as I ſhal be enabled. For, though it may come the more ſlowly forward, by reaſon of ſome lets: yet, I am perſwaded, God will ſupply, by his grace, whatſoeuer, I am that way depriued of. And (if I can haue patience) bring what I intend, to much more happie perfection,*

To the Reader.

perfection, then if I had receiued no obstacle in the performance.

This Psalme, *in the meane while, my friends were desirous of; and haue wished me thus to publish the rest, by one or two together, vntill a whole* Decade *be imprinted: That so (euery* Psalme, *being an entire thing of it selfe) those poore men, who are desirous of them, and vnable to spare so much money together, as will buy a greater booke, may by little and little, without any hinderance furnish themselues of all. And beside, they thinke the portablenesse of it, may make it the more frequently read; for which causes I haue hearkned vnto them.*

Take then in good part, this little beginning

To the Reader.

beginning. Value it, as it shall deserue to bee esteemed; And, let not my vnworthinesse bee any blemish vnto it. For, though I am no profest Diuine; yet, my profession is Christianitie, and these my labours, hauing the approbation of Authority, are not to be despisedly reckoned of, as mine; but receiued as the doctrines of the Church: *who hath now, by her allowance, both made them her owne, and deliuered them ouer vnto you. So; Gods blessing on you, and me, and farwell.*

G. W.

The feuerall Exercifes vpon this Pfalme,

are thefe.

1. A *Preamble*: wherein the *Author*, the *Perfon*, the *Matter*, the *Method*, the *Occafion*, and *Vfe*, of this Pfalme, are treated of. pag. 1.
2. The *Metricall Tranflation* of this Pfalme, with fhort notes, to iuftifie the queftionable places in that *verfion*. pag. 9.
3. The *Seuerall Readings* of this Pfalme, in moft of the ancient and moderne Interpreters. pag. 15.
4. An *Expofition*, diuided according to the parts of the Pfalme: the firft part begins, pag. 19. the fecond, pag. 89.
5. *Meditations in verfe*, vpon the fame Pfalme, beginning: pag 123.
6. A fhort Paraphrafe in profe, wherein the vvords of the Pfalme are vvholly preferued. pag. 159.
7. A Prayer, taken out of the Pfalme, petitioning for the bleffings; and to be deliuered from the vnhappineffe therein mentioned. pag. 163.

EXER-

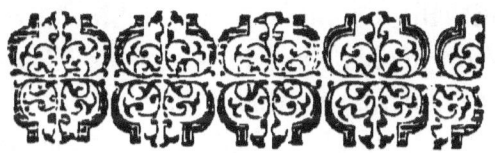

EXERCISES
VPON THE
firſt PSALME.

1. *Of the* Author *of the firſt Pſalme, and the perſon ſpeaking there: Of the* matter *alſo, and* method *of it: with the* occaſion, *and* vſe.

He firſt Pſalme (which hath no title in the *Hebrew*) moſt of the learned Fathers aſcribe to *Dauid*; as *Origen, Ambroſe, Baſil, Auguſtine, Caſsiodore,* &c. yea, and S. *Ierome* (though he elſewhere followeth

Exercises vpon

In Epist. ad Paulin de omnibus sacris Scripturis.	eth the opinion of the Hebrew Doctors in his time) in one of his * Epistles, attributes this *Psalme* to *Dauid*. Some also there bee, who suppose it to be composed by *Esdras*, who is affirmed by *Athanasius* and *Hylarie*, to haue gathered the *Psalmes* into one volume. But since the Scriptures make no certaine mention thereof, vrging no man to follow this or that opinion, I leaue it as indifferent; although I must confesse, that I myselfe am more enclined to their side, who impute this *Psalme*, with all the rest, to *Dauid*. But doubtles, whosoeuer it were, or by whomsoeuer the whole booke was thus ordered; this, was most properly made a Proeme to the rest, for that it treats of *Blessednesse*, which is the principall end of all Instructions.
The person speaking in the 1. Psalme, & the matters handled in it.	The *Person* principally speaking in this *Psalme*, is the *Holy Ghost*, by the mouth of the Prophet, who doth hereby

the firſt Pſalme.

hereby firſt teach vs who is truely happy, *verſ.* 1. 2. Secondly, by a Similitude, we are made to vnderſtand the excellent eſtate of him, that is ſo bleſſed. *verſ.* 3. And laſtly, wee are here informed, that the wicked being nothing ſo, dreame of a falſe vncertaine felicity, and are, both in reſpect of their preſent and future condition, moſt miſerable. *verſ.* 4. 5. 6. In breefe, this *Pſalme* may bee diuided into two parts, the firſt three verſes, ſet forth the bleſſedneſſe of the *Church* in *Chriſt,* and the other, declare the lamentable condition of all that ſeeke for happineſſe without him.

Something I will ſay, concerning the ground and occaſion of this *Pſalme*; for, I haue ſhown you before in my *Preparation*, that there were certaine diuine ſubiects, ſome of which the holy Prophet alwayes made the firſt *Obiects*, of his contemplations, — The occaſion of this Pſal.

Vide Prepar: to the Pſalter. cap. 5.

plations; and the meanes, whereby he afcended vnto the cleere knowledge of the high Myfteries, deliuered in euery *Pfalme*. Now, although here be no *Title* to fhew vs fo manifeftly, what he made the foundation of his contemplation, that we fhould peremptorily conclude it, to be this, or that particular; yet, by the matter of the *Pfalme*, we may (I hope) without iniury to the Holy Spirit, giue our meditations leaue to ayme therat. And to me it plainely appeareth to bee that Double-Law of God, which was giuen in *Paradife*. For, though at the beginning, God created man, that he fhould know, loue, enioy him, and bee made bleffed in that fruition; yet, he would not that fuch bleffedneffe fhould be obtained without fome condition. And therfore hee gaue him an eafie, but (as I fayd before) a Double-Law, partly affirmatiue, partly negatiue: the affirmatiue

Genef. 2.

The firſt Pſalme.

firmatiue part was, that hee ſhould dreſſe the garden, and eat freely of euery tree therein: the negatiue was, that he ſhould not eat of the Tree of knowledge of good and euill. And there was both a promise of reward, for his obedience; and a commination of puniſhment, if hee tranſgreſſed: but *Adam*, who by obedience, might haue beene eternally happy; by diſobedience, was thruſt out of *Paradiſe*, into a world of miſeries, to wander for euer in diſcontentment, and in the vnhappy ſhadowes of death. Which God beholding with pity, beſtowed on him, in place of originall righteouſneſſe which hee loſt; a meanes of Iuſtification: and (changing the accidents, though not the eſſence of his firſt command) gaue to him in his Word, that generall Law of Faith, by which hee, and his poſterity, might bee directed out of the way of perdition, and ariue

B 3 againe

againe at true felicity. This Myfteftery, being the firft in the holy book of God, that moft neerely concernes vs, the Prophet, as it feemeth, contemplated, and made it the obiect and ground-worke of this firft *Pfalme:* For, as God gaue to our firft *Parents* in *Paradife*, a negatiue and affirmatiue Law, fo in that vniuerfall Law, impofed fince their fall, fome things are commanded, and fome forbidden to bee done; and that Law, in refpect of the effence, is one throughout all the ages of the Church. Moreouer, as *Adam*, if hee had kept the Commandement of God in *Paradife*, fhould haue there liued a happy life, and peraduenture beene tranflated from thence without death, into a more glorious bleffedneffe in Heauen; fo wee, by keeping the Law, which is fince giuen vnto vs infteed of the Tree of life in this world, fhall obtaine the bleffedneffe

the firſt Pſalme.

neſſe of Grace in Gods Church for the preſent, and the perfection of all happineſſe (euen the life of eternall glory) hereafter. Contrariwiſe, as *Adam*, by contemning the Law of God, with the tree of life, in eating the forbidden fruit, loſt thereby the Eſtate of bleſſedneſſe, and incurred for the breach of a double Law, the danger of a double death; ſo, thoſe which tranſgreſſe the two-fold Law of Faith and Workes, which he hath ſince giuen in his Word, doe both depriue themſelues of the fore-named felicity, and are the ſecond time (and that irrecouerably) in the way of eternall damnation.

The effect hereof is opened in this *Pſalme*; and therefore it may with good probability bee ſuppoſed, that he tooke the Parable, whereupon he compiled this *Hymne*, from the Myſtery of the Tree of *Life* planted in *Paradiſe*, and from the Law and

Exercises vpon

Charge which was there giuen vnto *Adam*; and he sheweth, that as the transgression of the Commandement, is the way that perisheth; so the fulfilling of the *Law of the Lord*, is the onely meanes which is left vs, to recouer againe the happinesse that we haue lost.

The vse of this Psalme. This *Psalme* wee may sing, or meditate, when wee are disposed to praise and set forth the blessed and vnspotted life of our Redeemer; or else, when wee are discouraged with the prosperity of wicked worldlings (which seemes to bee the onely happy men) we may hence, both informe our selues of their end: and comfort our soules, with remembrance of the blessed estate, of a good Christian.

THE

The metricall Translation of
the first Psalme.

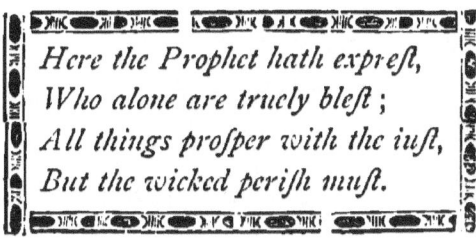

Here the Prophet hath exprest,
Who alone are truely blest;
All things prosper with the iust,
But the wicked perish must.

THe Man is ᵃ*blest, who walketh not* ᵇaftray
  In their ᶜlewd *Counsels, that ungodly are,*
Who neither standeth in the sinners way,
  Nor with the scornfull sitteth in their chaire.

But, in the Law of the ᵈeternall LORD,
  ᵉSincerely *placeth he, his whole delight,*
And in his Law, ᶠhis euer-blessed Word,
  Doth ᵍ*excercise himselfe both day and night.*
                                                        He,

He shall be like a tree, which close beside
    The ʰ *Riuers set, his fruit doth timely giue ;*
His leafe shall neuer fade, ⁱ *but fresh abide,*
    ᵏ*And whatsoe're he takes in hand shall thriue.*

But with ungodly men it is not so :   (fann'd)
    For they are like the chaffe, which   (¹ being
By puffs of winde, is driuen to and fro.
    In Iudgement, therfore shall not sinners stand:

*Nor the ungodly*ⁿ *(be admitted) where,*
    The righteous shall ᵒ*in one assemble*ᵖ *then :*
For, ᑫ*G*OD *well knowes their way yᵗ Righteous*
    But perish shall, yᵉ path of wicked men. (are

    ᵃ Blessings, or all happy things, belong to that man, &c. For some take the Hebrew word to be a Substantiue plurall, and some an Adiectiue plurall ; but which soeuer it be, it is fully enough expressed in this our English phrase, *Blest*, or, *Blessed is the man.* ᵇ The word, *astray*, seemes heere to be added onely for the verse sake, but the sence indeede includeth it, seeing it is an erroneous

The first Psalme.

ous walking from God, which is meant in this place. ᶜ This Epithite is not added in the Originall, nor other, which I somtime vse in my metricall translation of the Psalmes: neuerthelesse, I think I may, with a good conscience, insert them; where they are either such, as are warrantable in some other places of holy Scripture, to bee well vsed in that sence: or such as may bee naturally proper to the subject, which they are applyed vnto. As I thinke this is. ᵈ This word, *Eternall*, is an attribute most proper to God, and indeede not to be applyed to any other. For, nothing can be rightly called *eternall*, but that which euer *is*, *was*, and *shall bee*, without beginning or ending: and therfore I haue added it to the word, LORD, that it might the better expresse here, the Hebrew *Tetragrammaton*, יהוה᛫ ᵉ This, and many other such like words, may seeme to bee added in diuers places of my translation; whereas, the power of the Hebrew being considered, they will bee found included in the Text. ᶠ These words are added, *explicandi causâ*, and therefore put in a different character: which liberty, all Translators haue taken, euen in their prose-translations; and to authorize me heerein, I haue not onely the example of moderne Interpreters, but of the *Septuagint* also, who both *explicandi, & ornandi causâ*, haue added many words, in their translation. As in the fourth verse of this Psalme, ὀυκ ὄυτως, and in the second verse also, ἀπὸ προσώπευ τῦς γῆς, neither of which, are in the Hebrew. ᵍ The word, *exercise*, which is vsed in some English Translations, doth (in my opinion) better and more fully expresse the meaning of the Holy

Exercises vpon

Holy Ghost, then the word, *meditate*; seeing it may as properly bee applyed to the *heart* and *tongue*, as to the *hand*; whereas the word, *meditate*, is neuer with vs vsed so largely, although it be sometime so taken, with the *Latines*. ʰ *Riuers*, of it self, aswell expresseth the meaning of the Prophet in our tongue, as *Riuers of water*; for, as by *Flames*, without other addition, we vnderstand *Flames of fire:* so, without other addition also, by *Riuers*, we fully enough vnderstand, *the water, diuiding it selfe into many streames*. ⁱ These words are *explicandi causa* also, as that, spoken of before in the second verse. ᵏ *And he shall make what e're he doth to thriue;* so it may be read also; for some translate the words thus, *Et quicquid faciet, prosperare faciet.* ˡ *Explicandi causa*, as before. ᵐ In the first verse, because there are degrees of *Sinners* mentioned, and (in the Hebrew) distinguished by three seuerall words, which the *Latines* interpret *Impij, Peccatores*, and *Derisores*, that is, the *Vngodly, Sinners*, and *Scorners*, therefore in that, and in all such places, where is meant more then one sort of offenders, I haue called them, which the *Latines* terme *Impij*, the 𝔚𝔦𝔠𝔨𝔢𝔡, or 𝔘𝔫𝔤𝔬𝔡𝔩𝔶; and those which they call *Peccatores*, I haue termed 𝔖𝔦𝔫𝔫𝔢𝔯𝔰: but in this, and such like places (where one kinde of euill doers is onely spoken of) I haue indifferently named them, sometime the 𝔚𝔦𝔠𝔨𝔢𝔡, sometime the 𝔘𝔫𝔤𝔬𝔡𝔩𝔶, sometime 𝔖𝔦𝔫𝔫𝔢𝔯𝔰, and sometime by such other names, as I knew were vsuall in our tongue, to denote such Sinners, as the Holy Ghost there poynted at; for, howsoeuer the circumstances doe in many places appropriate these words, the 𝔖𝔦𝔫𝔫𝔢𝔯𝔰,

ᵐ *The direction letter is heere left out in the verse; and therfore refer this note to the word,* Sinners, *in the last verse of the fourth Stanza.*

the firſt Pſalme.

Sinners, or the **Ungodly**, to particular degrees of Offenders: yet in our tongue, we indifferently vſe either of them, to ſignifie the congregation of reprobate-members of the Deuill. ⁿ Theſe words are included in the ſenſe, though not literally expreſſed, *vide annotationes Franciſc. Vatabl.* ᵒ This is added, *explicandi cauſa*; for here ſeemes to be meant, that great Aſſembly of the Faithfull, which at the generall Iudgement, ſhall bee perfectly made *one* in Chriſt, who is the head of that myſticall body. ᵖ I may ſeeme perhaps, to haue inſerted this word, *then*, more for the rimes ſake, then for any force it here hath; but, being well conſidered, it will appear to be neceſſarily added, for it hath reſpect to the time of that iudgment (ſpoken of before) in which will be congregated that principall Aſſembly of the righteous, out of which all vnrepentent ſinners ſhall be vndoubtedly excluded. ᑫ I told you in my *Preparation to the Pſalter*, that where ſoeuer in tranſlating theſe Pſalmes, I met with the Hebrew *tetragrammaton* יהוה᛫ I would either expreſſe it by the word *LORD*, as the *Apoſtle*, the *Septuagint*, the *Fathers*, and ſome Engliſh tranſlators haue done; or elſe by ſuch a word as ſhould ſomewhat eſſentially expreſſe the Godhead: and diſtinguiſh it alſo by writing the ſame in Capitall letters; as in this place, the word *GOD* is Charactered: Which (how euer ſome may thinke) is a ſignificant, eſſentiall name of the Deitie; yea, (except the Hebrew *Tetragrammaton*, whoſe myſteries I am not able to ſearch into) I thinke there is no one word of any language, more ſignificant to expreſſe the eſſence of the Deitie, then

is

is the word *GOD*, which though it be for difference sake a little otherwise pronounced, is the same in signification with the word of *GOOD*, an English *tetragrammaton* (out of whose number and forme of letters, if it were to any purpose, I durst vndertake to gather mysteries equall to many of those which some Iewish Rabbines and Catalictical Doctors haue framed out of the letters and forme of the Hebrew *vnspeakeable Name*.) It comprehends in it selfe all attributes whatsoeuer, which are expressed in the knowne Names of God, vsed throughout euery language of the world, for eternity, omnipotency, beautie, knowledge, loue, prouidence, blessednes, with the perfection of these, and all other excellencies; serue but to make vp one *Summum Donum*, one Chiefe good, and that is *GOD:* who, is the perfection of all Goodnesse, and he, to whom onely this essentiall Name ought to be giuen. As appeareth in St *Matthews* Gospell, Chap. 19. vers. 17. where Christ himselfe telleth vs, that there is none to whom this name of GOOD, appertaines, but to the Deitie: *There is none good, but one*, sayth he, *euen God*. And this is made somewhat the plainer, by considering the english word, by which we signifie him that is Gods opposite; for, we call him not as other Nations doe, by a name comprehending some one attribute of his, as the *deceiuer*, or so; but we impose a name on him, which at once, expresseth all that can be said of him in a thousand words, to wit, the *Deuill*; for, all the particular vnhappinesses, mischiefes, and wickednesses of the world, put together, doe make but one perfect *euill*, and he in whom they meet is properly termed

med the *Deuil* or *th'euill*, for it so seemes to haue beene aunciently pronounced, vntill the Saxon Character being somewhat like our D. made vs loose their pronunciation ; and as we call him that is the fulnesse of all Good, G O D ; so; him that is the protection of all euill, wee name the *Deuill*. *These notes I haue added, to shew the Reader, that in my transtation I tooke no vaine libertie, but made conscience of the least variation, and passed ouer nothing, vntill I had some reasonable warrant for what I did.*

Variæ Lectiones.

Ver 1. *Musculus, & translationes Anglicanæ reddiderunt in* præsenti, *sed Græcus, & Latina vulgata, & reliqui, tā veteres, quàm recentiories, legunt in* preterito; *& alijhabent* accedit ad consiliũ, *alij* ambulauit in consilia, *pretera Grec: vertit* ἐπὶ καθεδρα λοιμοῦ. *i.* in sede Pestilentiarũ, *vt est, in vulg: lat: sed Ieronim: habet*, Cathedra deriforum, *sic est etiam in recentioribus.*

Ver. 2. Deliciæ ipsius, *recentior:* voluntas

luntas eius in lege domini, *vulgat: lat.* In lege Iehovæ: *recentior:* in ftatuto, *Chaldeus.* *Pluraliter* in ftatutis, *Arabs: intelligens quæuis inftituta Dei.* *& vbi eft,* in lege eius meditabitur *in vulg: lat: tranflatio Anglicana nouifsima, & alij habent,* Meditatur, *& Chaldeus,* in luminatione eius cantat, *five* Iubilat.

Ver. 3. Et eft velut, *&c. alij legunt,* & fuit, *Græcus* κὶ ἔσται, *i.* & erit. Quæ fructum fuum dat: *recentior:* dabit *Genev:* fructum fuum concoquens, ad maturitatem producens, *Chaldeus.* Folium eius non marcefcit, *recentior:* non defluet, *Vulg. Lat.* & omnia, quæcunque faciet, profperabuntur, *Vulg. Lat. Chaldæus fic reddidit,* Omne germen quod germinat, grauefcit, & profperatur.

Ver. 4. Non fic Impij *recentiores.* *Sic eft etiam in Vulgat: Lat. & in Septuagint. fed idem repetunt, vidt:* οὐκ οὕτως οἱ ἀσεβεῖς οὐκ οὕτως. Non fic impij, non fic,

the firſt Pſalme.

ſic, & *in fine verſus addunt*, ἀπὸ προ-σώπου τῆς γῆς, à facie terræ. *Sic etiam & Arabs.* Tanquam gluma *recenti:* Puluis, *Vulgat. Lat. ſed idem ſignificat. nos enim in occidentali parte Angliæ vocamus tegumentum tritici,* 𝕯𝖚𝖘𝖙.

Ver. 5. Non ſtabunt impij *recenti: alij legunt,* Conſiſtent, *Græcus,* οὐκ ἀνα-στήσου], Non reſurgunt. *Sic Vulgat. Lat.* In iudicio, *recent:* in Die Iudicij magni, *Chaldæus.* In fine, *Arabs: denotans extremum Iudicium, in fine Mundi.* In Congregatione Iuſtorum *recenti. Alij* in Cætu. *Alij* in Concilio. *Græc:* οὐκ βουλῇ δικαίων. *Vulg: Lat:* In Conſilio Iuſtorum.

Nota, quod in libris Græcis & Latinis, verſus tertius in duos diuiditur.

The reaſon why I haue heere inſerted theſe various Readings, and in Latine, rather then in Engliſh, appeares in the third chapter of my Preparation to the Pſalter.

C   The

The first part of the PSALME.

1. *Blessed is the man, that doth not walke in the counsell of the vngodly, nor stand in the way of sinners, nor sit in the seat of the scornfull.*

2. *But his delight is in the Law of the* LORD, *and in his Law doth he meditate, day and night.*

3. *And he shall bee like a tree planted by the riuers of waters, that will bring forth her fruit in season, his leafe shall not fade, and whatsoeuer he doth, shall prosper.*

The Expoſition.

In nomine Patris, & Filij, & Spiritus Sancti.

BLESSED: As a word of comfort, and a ſigne of good ſpeede to my labours, ſtands heere to make happy my beginning of this endeauor: and I humbly beſeech the Euer-liuing God of *Dauid*, both to make *bleſſed* my proceedings, & grant that my end may be crowned with the glorious reward, of eternall *Bleſſednes*. For, that is the precious Iewell, which euer ſince the world begun, hath beene the principall ayme, whereat euery man ſhot, and the prize, after which they haue run. But indeede, the way it hath beene often miſtaken, and among the *Philoſophers*, which were accounted wiſeſt, it was a long time queſtionable

<small>The way of Bleſſedneſſe, is by moſt men miſtaken.</small>

ble, both wherein this happinesse consisted, and by what meanes it was to bee attained vnto. Nor in the times of heathen ignorance onely, were men deceiued in their aymes; but euen amongst vs also, at this day, the greatest part run wide, proposing vnto themselues, a happinesse in the enioying of those vaine things, wherby, they are often hurried quite beside it. For, some place their felicity, or *Summum Bonum*, in hauing the soueraignty and authority ouer others; some, in abundance of riches; and the greatest part, Epicure-like, in fleshly delights and pleasures, *Let vs eat and drinke* (say they) *for to morrow we shall die.* But the Kingdome of God is not meat and drinke, as the Apostle saith; and therfore that men might not still bee deceiued, and so weary themselues in a wrong course; the Author of this Psalme hath here decided the matter in question: and shewes

In what things the Worldling placeth his happinesse.

1 *Cor.* 15.

Rom. 14. 17.

The first Psalme.

shewes vs, that true *Blessednesse*, neither consisteth in obseruation of the mortall vertues, as *Philosophers* thought; nor in the worship of many Gods, as the *Pagans* suppose; nor in obseruing the Law of *Moses*, as the *Iewes* dreame; nor in enioying the pleasures of this life, as great *Courtiers* and *Epicures* beleeue: But quite ouerthrowing the opinions of all these, and their foolish expectations, who build their contentment on honour, riches, and such like things of this world; he affirmes, that man only to be most truely blessed, and in the path to highest happinesse, who, shunning the wayes of meere naturall men, endeauoureth also to auoyd the custome of sinners, to seperate himselfe from the scornfull enemies of the truth, and to continue sincerely, embracing and rightly professing the doctrine of Gods word. And this kind of *Preface*, the Holy Ghost, as

Why the Holy Ghost vsed this preface.	as it seemes, hath vsed; because, by discouering (at the first view) so precious a Iewell, as *Blessednesse*; hee would allure men, to giue the more heede vnto those mysteries and instructions, which are afterward deliuered: and, if it were possible, make them more willingly conforme themselues vnto the courses, which are inclusiuely propounded. The like kind of beginning hath the heathen Philosopher, *Aristotle*, vsed in his *Ethicks*; and which is more to be heeded, our Sauiour made it the *Exordium* of his Doctrine: as appears in that his first Sermon preached in the Mount, where he begins to pronounce, who are blessed: *Blessed*
Matth. 5. 3.	
	(saith he) *are the peace makers, Blessed the poore in spirit, Blessed the meeke*, &c. and so saith our Prophet. *Blessed*, that is, according to the originall, *Blessednesse, Blessings*, or all happy things, *appertaine vnto that man, who walketh not*

the firſt Pſalme.

not in the Counſell of the vngodly, nor ſtandeth in the way of ſinners, as it followeth in the Pſalme. And this his *Bleſſedneſſe* is double ; for, he hath the hope and means of happineſſe in this world, and aſſurance of eternall glory in the next : or, as the Apoſtle expreſſeth it, *both the promiſe of this life, and that which is to come.* 1 *Tim.* 4. 8.

Now, what the bleſſings of this life are (which God hath ordained, for ſuch as walke in his ordinances) you may read in the laſt booke of *Moſes* ; *Bleſſed,* ſayd he, *ſhalt thou be in the Citie, and bleſſed in the field* ; *bleſſed ſhall be the fruit of thy body, the fruit of thy ground, the fruit of thy cattell, the encreaſe of thy kine, and the flocks of thy ſheep. Bleſſed ſhall bee thy basket, and thy ſtore* ; *bleſſed ſhalt thou be when thou goeth out, and bleſſed when thou com-meſt in.* Yea, as it is in the ſame chapter, among many other temporall bleſſings, *God ſhall make thee holy vnto himſelfe,* *Deut.* 28. 3.

himſelfe, if thou keepe his Commandements. Or if you would, in a word, receiue a glimpſe of the perfection of the bleſſedneſſe, which belongs to the godly man. *S. Paul* giueth vs the beſt knowledge of it, in ſhewing how farre it is beyond the reach of our knowledge; for, ſaith he, *neither hath eye ſeene, nor eare heard, nor can it enter in the heart of man, what God hath prepared for them that loue him,* 1 Cor. 2. 9.

This *Pſalme,* as I ſayd in the Argument, conſiſteth of two parts; in this firſt part, is ſet forth the bleſſed eſtate of the Iuſt, and who is ſuch an one: in the other part, the miſerable condition of the wicked. In the two firſt verſes, the *Bleſſedneſſe,* and Piety of the man ſo happy, is both negatiuely, and affirmatiuely deſcribed; for, the *Prophet* hath begun, according to that ſaying of *S. Peter, Shun euill, and doe good:* and indeed, true righteouſ-

[margin: 1 Cor.]
[margin: 1 Pet. 3. 11. Pſal. 34. 14.]

the first Psalme.

righteousnesse consisteth, aswell in eschewing what may prouoke, or displease God, as it is expressed in the first verse; as in seriously performing, or endeauouring that which may please him (which is declared in the second.) And, as a well experienced Physician, doth first purge away all the ill humours, that occasioned the sicknesse of his weake Patient; before hee will administer those Cordials, which are prepared to recouer his health: So, by this order, in his description of a blessed man, the Holy Ghost doth shew vs, that before the physick of his Word, can worke effectually in our hearts, for the saluation of our soules; wee must bee clensed from the corruptions, which wee haue gotten by the euill-affected *counsells* of our owne hearts, or, the infectious society of the wicked: and, as it were, diet our selues, by abstaining from their abhominable

minable customes; which *Dict,* is here first prescribed in the negatiue; And it is, as if hee had sayd thus. *If you euer intend to recouer the health of your soules, and become partakers of true blessednesse; you must neither walk in the counsels of the vngodly, nor stand in the way of sinners, nor sit in the seat of the scornfull:* for these are the courses which hee shuns, that doth arriue at *happinesse.*

What manner of expression the Holy Ghost vseth.

But, the Holy Ghost hath not here vsed the ordinary manner of speech, in his description; but rather, by way of *Metaphor,* exprest it: & the Diuine *Muse,* hath into three *Traids,* or triple heads, diuided this *Negatiue.* In which are to bee considered three *subicĕts,* three *qualities,* three *actions.* And there is an admirable *gradation* in all the parts: first, in the *subicĕts,* or *persons;* from an *vngodly man,* to a *sinner:* from a *sinner,* to a *scorner.* Next, in the *degrees* of sinne; as, from the

the *counsell*, to the *way*: from the *way*, to the *seat*. Lastly, in the *manner* of it; from *walking*, to *standing*; from *standing*, to *sitting*: and their wickednesse, is increased to the full.

By the *vngodly*, such are heere vnderstood, who are still in their originall corruptions; and being ignorant of God, and his seruice, encline to those euill affections, whereunto their nature is subiect. Yea, by the *vngodly*, are principally meant *Infidels*; such as are ignorant of religion, and the diuine worship of God, according to his Word: such, as employ all their endeauours, without thought of him, to become happy in this life; giuing themselues ouer vnto couetousnesse, pleasures, with such like vanities, whereunto their affections lead them.

The word *vngodly*, in our tongue, doth of it selfe, very well answer to this Explication; for, as *Godlinesse* most

The first Triade. The vngodly, who they are.

moſt properly appertaineth to *God* and *Faith*; ſo, *vngodlineſſe* expreſſeth the contrary thereunto. The Originall importeth ſuch a crue, as are ſo reſtleſly affected with worldly cares; and euill perturbations of the minde, that they are endleſly, hurried to and fro in their vngodlineſſe: like the ſea, which hath no power to ſtay it *Iſa.* 57. 20. ſelfe. And ſo *Eſay* deſcribes them, *The vngodly* (faith hee) *are like the troubled ſea, when it cannot reſt; whoſe waters caſt vp mire and dirt.*

Walking.

By *walking*, is Metaphorically vnderſtood, the ordinary proceeding *Pſal.* 119. 1. of men in all their actions, whether *Gen.* 5. 24. of faith or works. And in this place 2. *Chron.* 22. 3. is ment, a *departure* from God in the progreſſe of their liues. And although in my *metricall* tranſlation, I haue expreſſed it by adding the word, *aſtray*; it is nothing from the naturall ſence of the verſe: ſeeing there is ment an, erronius *walking*, or wandering

the first Psalme.

ring from the right way; as the word *abijt* in the vulgar latine, verie well manifesteth: for, it signifieth most properly, *to goe away*. And Saint *Augustine* faith, *Ille abijt, qui recessit a Deo.*

By *Councels* are here ment the internall deliberations of the minde; and that naturall inclination of man to euill, which God spake of when hee said; that the *Imaginations of the thoughts of his heart, were onely euill continually*. For, *Councell* is not here so strictly taken as *Aristotle* defines it in his *Ethicks*; where hee faith, that *Councell is the finding out of the fittest meanes to bring any thing to passe*; but *Councell* in this place, signifieth rather Tempations, then such Councell: and it hath aswell respect to the inward perswasions of our owne lusts, as to the outward aduise of others. *Euery man*, faith Saint *Iames, is tempted, when he is drawne away and enticed*

	Councell.
	Gen. 6. 5.
	Gen. 8. 21.
	*Arist.*3.*Eth.*3.
	Iam. 1. 4

Exerciſes vpon

ced by his owne corruption, *Iam.* 1. 4. But if you will know further, and more particularly what the externall *Councels* of the ungodly be, whereto they tend, and what euents follow them; you may reade it in the *Prouerbs* of *Solomon, Chap.* 1. *verſ.* 10. 2. *Sam.* 19. 2. *Gen.* 37. *&c.*

Triade 2.

Now, we come to the ſecond *Triade,* in the Negatiue, which ſaith; that the *Bleſſed* man, is ſuch a one as doth not *ſtand in the way of ſinners,* and here is expreſſed a degree of wickedneſſe beyond *walking in the Councels of the vngodly.* For, by thoſe that are ſaid to *ſtand* in the way of ſinners, are ſuch vnderſtood; who are not onely led by the vaine deuiſes, and imaginations of their owne hearts (which proceede from original guiltines) or ſuch, who are ſimply ignorant of God, and Religion (as the heathen nations are) But, thoſe are thereby ment alſo, who haue follow-

Sinners who they are.

the first Psalme.

lowed the *Councell* of their owne lusts, to put them in execution, with such as are willingly ignorant of the worship of God; negligent of the meanes of their conuersion: and offendors against the precepts of the first, and second Table of the law. These are said to *stand*, not because they walke no further in the path of vnrighteousnesse: but rather, because they not returning back to the way of Godlinesse, follow their wicked actions, with a setled delight in them: *Stant quia in peccato delectantur*, saith Saint *Augustine*; yea, they are such as perseuere vntill they haue gotten a habit in sinne, and made (as it were) a beaten path in vnrighteousnesse. For, such is the *Emphasis* of the word, as it imports a *continuance* and *insisting* in euill: not a falling by infirmitie, as *Dauid*, and *Peter* fell; but a reiterating and heaping of sinne vpon sinne, through the whole course of their liues.

To stand, what it meanes.

Exercises vpon

liues. For, the word *way*, both here, and in other places of Scripture is many times Metaphorically vſed for Doctrine, or Religion ; and ſometimes for the manner of our liuing, whether good or bad. But, the *way* that the *Prophet* here meanes, is that *broade and much troden way, leading to destruction*, whereof our Sauiour ſpake, in the Goſpell of Saint *Matthew*.

And to make the matter more plaine ; thoſe that *ſtand in the way of Sinners*, are not ſuch as vnwilling, or through infirmity offend : For, *there is no man on the earth that doth good, and ſinneth not* (ſaith the Preacher) but thoſe who ſetling there loue vpon euill, haue gotten (as I ſaid) a habit in ſinning : and ſuffer themſelues to bee carried headlong by the concupiſcence of their hearts into all wicked actions, vntill they haue by continuance made themſelues

---

What the way is,
Pſal. 86. 11.
Acts. 18. 25.

Ma. 7. 13.

Eccles. 7. 22.

Who they are that ſtand in the way of Sinners.

the first Pfalme. 33

felues not onely feruants to finne and vncleanneffe: but euen blufhleffe, and without fhame, both of what they doe; or before whom, they commit their follies.

Such, were the *Sodomites*, that preffed into the houfe of *Lot*; fuch finners, were the *Beniamites* of *Gibeah*; fuch, are all the keepers of publick houfes of iniquity; fuch, are thofe common fwearers; that when you tell them of their oathes, will in fport (to make an vnfauory ieaft) fweare that they fwore not: fuch, are they, that goe to bed late, and rife early, to follow drunkenneffe; fuch, are thofe that fpend all their youth in ridiculous vanities, and are diftinguifhed from the children of God, by their language; For, it often foundeth *God damme me*; and fuch, are thofe Gallants amongft vs, as dare, impudently, boft of their beaftlineffe, or in merriment publifh their

Gen 19. 4.
Iud. 19. 22.

Efay. 5. 11.
Pro. 23. 29.

D   owne

Exercises vpon

Gen. 13. 13.
Sam. 15. 18.
Math. 26. 45.
Luke 7. 37.
Iob. 9. 16.

The 3. Triad.

What it is to fit in the feate of the fcornefull.

Scorners who they are.

owne lafciuioufneffe: euen thefe are fuch, as the holy-Ghoft meaneth in this *Triade*; and diftinguifheth from other offendors, by the name of *finners*; as appeareth through both *Teftaments*.

The laft part, or *Triade* of this Negatiue is: hee muft not *fit in the feate of the fcornefull* (that is) hee muft not haue fellowfhip with obftinate Hereticks; nor careflefly, ftubbornly, or againft his owne knowledge, continue in vnrighteoufnes or vnbeleefe: nor fcoffe at Religion, with the profeffors thereof: nor infult ouer good men in their miferies: nor by blafphemous fpeeches, or erronious doctrines, malicioufly oppofe himfelfe againft God, and his truth: nor be affociated with fuch men, as are wholly giuen ouer to a reprobate fenfe. For, by *fcorners*, the holy Ghoft meanes thofe, who are not only guilty of originall vncleaneneffe;
or

the first Psalme.

or polluted with actuall sins; but so rooted in them, that they haue there, set vp their rest; yea, they are such as, being hardned by their continuance in sinne, grow incorrigible, incredulous of Religion, contemners of God, and so presumptuous; as they dare reproach, blaspheme him, peruert his truth against their owne knowledges; and yet as it were in despite of him, promise vnto themselues impunity: Such they are also, as vngraciously deride the ordinance of God; and make Iests at his word. And such, Saint *Peter* said, there should be in the last dayes; euen *scoffers, walking after their owne lusts, and saying, where is the promise of his comming: for, since the Fathers fell asleepe, all things continue as they were?* Such *sinners,* and *scorners* as these; were the *Iewes* that despised *Christ*: Such, are they that for temporall aduancements, maintaine Doctrines against

Pet. 3. 3.

36	*Exercises vpon*

Mat. 23. 14.

The Chaire or seate of Scorners.

To *sit*; what it meanes.

the knowne truth, and their owne Confciences; fuch, are thofe that make Religion a colour for their villany; *Deuouring widowes houfes, vnder the pretence of long prayer*: and thefe, if they once get into the *Chaire*, and fit there; are thofe finners which fhall neuer bee forgiuen: For, by the *Chayre*, or *feate*, is vnderftood; a defperat fecurity, and a diuelifh obftinacy in malicious wickedneffe; and hee is properly faid to *fit* there, that continues in his peruerfeneffe, without repentance, vnto the end of his life. And the reafon why there is no redemption for fuch, is; not becaufe there is want of mercy in God: but by reafon there is no repentance in man.

Thefe, make vp the three *degrees* of comparifon, and the third and laft ftep to the Diuell: For, to *walke* in the *councell* of the *vngodly* (which is the purpofe of finning) is bad: To *ftand*

The first Psalme. | 37

stand in the *way* of *sinners* (which is the action of it) is worse; But to *sit* in the *seate* of the *scornefull* (which is to die impenitent in his wickednesse) is worst of all, and the highest degree of a Reprobate.

But, to draw into fewer words this expofition of thefe three-folde Negatiues; by the *vngodly*, are ment *vnbleeuers*; by *sinners*, thofe that are vniuſt and difhoneſt in their actions; by *scorners*, obſtinate Hereticks; by the *Councels of the vngodly*, are vnderſtood the vaine cogitations of meere naturall men, with the fuperſtitions of *Iewes* and *Pagans*; the *way of sinners*, is a vitious courfe of life, as the breach of the morrall precepts; and the *Chayre of Scorners*, is the obſtinate profeſſion of falfe Doctrines. Now, he that beleeues not the promife of the Gofpell, *walkes* in the *Councell* of the firſt; hee that addicts himfelfe to Pride, Couetouſneſſe

<small>A briefe of what went before.</small>

D 3

Exercises vpon

neffe and fuch like; *ftands* in the *way* of the fecond: And hee, that dies in the maintenance of a falfe worfhip, or in any of thefe finnes, without repentance; is feated in the *feate* of the *fcornefull*. Which the *Septuagint* calleth; the *Chaire of Peftilence*. And it very well expreffeth the nature of that finne: For, as the plague of Peftilence, is a difeafe moft dangerous; infectious; and the fuddaine deuourer of mightie congregations: So, thofe kind of finners doe by their doctrines, contemptible fpeeches of God, and euill example; quickly infect, poyfon, and kill the foules of an innumerable multitude of men. And therefore, obftinate Hereticks, Atheifts, falfe Teachers, Scorners of the Truth, Deriders of Religion, and vnrepentent finners; may very well be faid to fit, in the *Chayre of Peftilence*: For, they are the plague of the world; and to be abhorred as a moft

Marginal note: The Chaire of Peftilence.

most dangerous, and infectious Pestilence, to the soule of Man.

And thus haue you this gradation opened; which may bee eyther vnderstood according, to the ordinarie course: to wit, as from the positiue, to the superlatiue: in this manner. He that is a blessed man, must bee carefull, that he *walke not in the Councell of the vngodly*; much more that he *stand not in the way of sinners*: but aboue all things, he must be most circumspect, that he shunne; *the infectious seate of Scorners*; Or, else it may be inuerted thus: The man that wold be blessed; ought not only to auoide *the pestilent seate of Scorners* & obstinnate inrepentant sinners: but eschew also as farre asin him lies, *the action, or iteration of any sinne*; nay, he should not so much as suffer his thoughts willingly, to wander after *the vngodly persvvasions of carnall desires*.

The *Doctrines* and *Obseruations*,

The Doctrines & Obseruations arising out of this verse.
Ob. 1.

which may properly be gathered out of this verse, are these. First, I obserue, that there be but three steps to Hell, the *purpose* of sinne; the *action* of it; and an *obstinate continuance* therein, without repentance: and vnlesse we be very watchfull, we may slip downe those three stayres, before we be aware: For, *Facilis descensus Auerni*; it is an easy way to Hell: and the nature of sinne is such; that it infinuates by degrees, into the heart, without being perceiued. First, it serues into good liking; and gaines the consent, or purpose; then proceedes it vnto action. And so forward, vntill it grow ripe; euen to the contempt of God: and this is the policy of the Diuell; to deceiue men: For hee knowes, if hee should perswade at first onset, to renounce God: it is so vnnaturall a sinne; that it wold seem abhominable, to the worst disposed men: & the hart would not admit

The policy of the Diuell, to draw vs vnto the Counsels of the vngodly, and so forth to destruction.

the firſt Pſalme.

admit ſuch a perſwaſiō to take place. Therefore, he makes not that appeare to bee his ayme ; but preſents them, rather with ſuch bayts, as ſeeme to haue no danger in them. He counſels them (according to the natural enclination of their hearts, and the example of worldlings) to ſeeke preferments, riches, pleaſures, with ſuch like vanities ; hee ſhewes them the glory and vſe they may haue ; he perſwades the Chriſtian, who is in a meane degree of life, that if he would ſeeke after honours, he might thereby become a Patron, for the afflicted members of the Church, or Common-wealth. But he knowes well, the olde ſaying will proue true, *Honores mutent mores*, Honours change manners : and that preferment is able, not onely to make them forget many good thoughts, and reſolutions, which they haue in a lower eſtate : but to blot out of memory alſo :

alſo, friendſhip, kinred, and the knowledge of themſelues (as wee daily ſee it doth) yea, the Deuill is ſure, that if hee can procure a man, but once to climb the ladder of promotion; it will ſo intangle him with the loue thereof, that it is twenty to one, but that he will renounce God, before hee will yeeld to ſtep one degree backe againe.

Others, hee tempts with eaſe; and makes them (poore ſoules) beleeue, that if they might disburthen themſelues of ſuch buſineſſes, or ſuch and ſuch cares, that they ſhould then better attend to the ſeruice of God, and with a more quiet minde, follow their deuotions. But the Decciuer is ſubtill, and hath by experience ſeene, that afflictions make thoſe ſeek God, often and earneſtly, that being deliuered of their cares, cannot finde one houre in a month, to ſerue him.

Others, againe, hee allureth with the

The firſt Pſalme. 43

the loue of riches: and that hee may may do ſo, he cauſeth them to imagin (perhaps) that if they were wealthy, as ſome men are, whom they know: there ſhould not ſo many poore people, goe thinly clad; nor ſuch numbers die, for want of ſuſtenance. So many *Churches* ſhould not lie ruined; nor ſo many works of *Pietie*, or for the publike profit, bee vnperformed. Yea, he perſwades them, that theſe temporall things, may not only be ſought after, and enioyed, without the diſpleaſure, or diſhonour of God; but ſerue him alſo for his ſeruice, and the better ſetting forth of his glory. And indeed, ſo they may; where they are moderately ſought after, and gained by honeſt meanes. But, where there is one that ſeekes them, with ſuch temperance; there are ten, who ſettle their mindes ſo vpon them, as they choke up all theſe good determinations, that were

Few ſeeke the things of this world temperately, as they ought.

were at firſt ſpringing in their hearts. For, a man that is not contented with his eſtate, but deſires things out of his owne concupiſcence, without reſpect vnto the will of God; that man hath giuen the Deuill aduantage, and is *walking in the counſells of the vngodly*; euen after the vaine cogitations of an vnregenerate heart. And not conſidering the dangerous aduiſe, that his appetite giues him; hee firſt ſuffers his thoughts, to bee buſied about thoſe vanities; next, approoues of them; and then haſtens, to put them in execution: which aduantage, the Enemy of mans ſafety hauing gotten, hee cauſeth him to iterate, and augment his tranſgreſſion, vntill his heart growes hardned, and his conſcience loſe the ſence and feeling of ſinne.

And ſo it comes to paſſe, that hee, who made no account of the tranſitory things of this life, and was touched

the first Pfalme. 45

ched with the guilt of such, as the world accounts most veniall sinnes; before he was allured vnto the *Counsells of the ungodly*: having *walked* a little in them; steps suddenly into the *way of sinners*. Which is a great broad path, that leades downe a steepe hill, vntill (without the great mercy of God) he ariue at the *seat of the scornfull*, or the chaire of obstinate impenitency: and when hee is once so low, and seated there; the hill of repentance prooues so steep, that hee neuer returnes again; but there continueth in a desperate estate.

Hereby then wee are taught, that if wee will bee preserued from the danger of sinne, we must auoyd the custome of sinne; yea, the first enticements, & least occasions thereof; and not presume vpon our owne strength: for, hee that is content to heare euill *counsell*, tempts God; and is not sure, whether he will therefore draw

Doct.

draw his grace from him, and suffer him to bee deluded by it. Concupiscence; if it be not resisted, will turne to action; action, to iteration; and at last, comes hardnesse of heart: for, he that feeles in himselfe, the euill motions of lust, and can hardly restraine them, hauing no obiects to entice him; how much lesse, will he bee able to curb them, if hee come, where hee may haue the beauty, and wantonnesse of another, to inflame him? Or, if he could not bridle his affections before he had committed vncleannesse, when hee had more grace, more shame, more denials, and many more stops, to hold him backe, from wickednesse: Alas! why should any man thinke it possible, for him to forsake it, at his owne pleasure, when hee hath put himselfe out of the way of vertue; and hath neither inward grace, nor outward meanes, to preuent it? If, when thou hadst two eyes,

the firſt Pſalme.

eyes, thou couldſt not keep the way, being in it: canſt thou hope, hauing neuer an eye left thee; to find it, when thou art out of it? No doubtleſſe, if wee cannot keepe the ſea from ouer-flowing vs, when the bankes are whole; ſurely, after they are once broken, the breach will encreaſe, and the flouds will come in, vntill they haue quite ouer-whelmed vs: vnleſſe the mercifull hand of a greater power, then our owne, help to recouer vs. A little water will extinguiſh a cole; but a flame is not ſo eaſily quenched. And therefore, we ought to kill theſe Cockatrices in the egge, and bee wary, not to giue the leaſt advantage, vnto the infirmities of euill. We haue examples enough to warne vs. *Dauid* was a good, and an extraordinary man; yet, giuing his eyes too much liberty, the euill *counſells* of vngodly affections, got by thoſe windowes, into his heart, and drew him on on in their *walke*, vntill they brought him to the *way of sinners*; where hee *stood* a long time, heaping one offence vpon another: And had not God sent a *Prophet* of purpose, to call him out of that *way*; as holy a man as he was, he had neuer of himselfe returned, vntill he had taken vp his *seat with the scorners*. And yet, for all this, wee, euen wee weaklings, dare giue our selues any liberty. We can willingly runne thither, where wee know before, that we shall here see; nay, bee compelled, to bee partakers of sinne: and notwithstanding, warrant our owne safeties.

The bold presumption of man.

Some, I haue heard say; that in all companies, they could beare themselues temperately, and among Drunkards, escape free, though all their companie failed of that gouernment: but alas, they see not their owne deformities; for, I haue knowne, that some of them, were euen

the first Psalme.   49

uen then distempered, when they sayd so.

Others, I haue heard, so confident in their owne vertues; that they haue professed themselues able, to resist the strongest temptations of incontinency: and that, though they were all alone, with the most tempting beauty, and where they had the greatest prouocations to folly; they could neuerthelesse keep themseues, from any dishonest act. This I haue heard: and beleeue me; I think such a thing possible, if they rely more on Gods grace, then their owne abilities; and came into this temptation, by accident, without wilfull seeking, or desiring any such occasion. Yea, many (no doubt) haue escaped such trials. But, if any man depend vpon his owne chastity, and purposely tempt himselfe with opportunities, to doe euill; hee, walkes *the way* which God approoues not: and therefore it shall
E perish.

perish; yea, although hee intended, at the first, no more, but to haue it in his power, to doe euill; it is a thousand to one, if God giue him not ouer, to be vanquished by that sinne, which hee foolishly presumed to ouercome.

Genef. 39.

Whilst *Ioseph* was about his businesse, the allurements of his Mistres had no power ouer him: and so, whilst with him, we seek well to employ our selues; though *counsels of vngodlines*, be rounded in our eares; and strange vnlooked for temptations, with faire opportunities, lay siege against vs; yet they shall not preuaile; no, not these that seeme Mistresses ouer our affections, and powerfull enough to command vs. But, if we leaue to be honestly busied, and, as many of vs young men doe, being idle our selues, seeke out those, who are euery way as idle; and with vaine discourse, or vnseemly gestures,

passe

The first Pſalme.

paſſe away our precious houres. Queſtionleſſe, ſomtime or other, we ſhall bee betrayed to commit that, which wee little thought perhaps, to haue beene guilty of; and grow, after a while, ſo baſe, to ſeeke that thing of the *May'd*, which wee preſumed the *Miſtreſſe* could neither haue commanded, not wooed vs vnto. Nay, I am perſwaded; that *Ioſeph*, who hath gotten the title of Chaſte: if hee would haue left his affaires, and ventured himſelfe, as ſome of vs doe, in effeminate court-ſhips; it is to be feared, that the Spirit of God would haue left him, as it forſook *Sampſon*, or *Dauid*. And then, a meaner woman then his *Miſtreſſe*, might haue wrought him to her will; and it is a queſtion, whether he would not haue proued the Attempter, of hers, or ſome others Chaſtity.

The ſecond obſeruation, that wee may take from hence, is this; that if *Obſer.* 2.

there bee degrees in sinne, and seuerall steps, that lead vs from the way of blessednesse; we must not thinke it enough, if we can auoyd some one degree of sinne. Nay, it is not sufficient, if we shun all but one: for, he that hath gone but one step backe from the right way; if hee doe not come backe that one step, he is neuer likely to ariue at happinesse, though hee neuer goe further on in a wrong path. But it is impossible, to stay vpon any one degree of sinning (without repentance) and not to step into another: as appeareth in the former obseruation.

Obser. 3.

Two sorts of men, heee warned to repent.

Thirdly, if wee must bee wary, to auoyd the *Counsels of the vngodly*, & the impiety of misbeliefe; aswel as to shun *the way of sinners:* which (as I sayd before) is the committing of actuall sinnes. Then, two sorts of men are hereby warned, to amend themselues, if they euer will intend to bee blessed:

the first Psalme.

blessed: The first, are those morall men, that thinke it sufficient, so they can bee counted iust pay-masters, quiet neighbours, honest plaine-dealers, and such as doe no men hurt; though they neuer know what belongs to God, or Religion. The other, are such Professors, as suppose; that if they haue heard Diuine Seruice, twice euery Saboth; six Lectures in a week; and slubbered ouer their ordinary deuotions: it is no matter, how dishonestly they liue; how vncharitable, and contentious they be among their neighbours; nor how irregular they bee in the courfe of their liues. But, both these ought to know, that God promiseth not any *Blessednesse* to such Triflers, as do his seruice by halues; but vnto them, that hauing both *religion*, and *honesty*; *faith*, and *workes*; neither *walke in the Counsels of the vngodly: nor stand in the way of sinners.* For, all others are

Exercises vpon

in danger, to take vp their *seat* with the *scornfull*.

Verse 2.

Thus much, of the *Blessed* mans description, by the *Negatiue*, contained in the first verse of this *Psalme*. On which I wil enlarge my obseruations no further; but come to the *Affirmatiue*, contained in these words. *But his delight, is in the Law of the* LORD, *and in his Law, doth hee meditate day and nigh.*

Three things obseruable in the second verse.

In which *Affirmatiue*, there are three things to bee obserued, by the blessed man; & they are opposed to those three, which are to be auoyded in the former verse: To the *walking in the Counsells of the vngodly*, is opposed, *a delight in the Law of the* LORD: to *standing in the way of sinners*, is opposed, *the meditation of the Diuine Word*: and, to *sitting in the seat of the scornfull*, a continuall *perseuerance, both day and night, in the true seruice of God.* Yea, these words haue

in

the firſt Pſalme.

in them, an excellent *Antitheſis*, or contradiction, to the courſes of the wicked; who, employeth al his counſels, endeauours, and actions, in ſeeking vaine ends, and aduancing his owne wayes: while the iuſt man, ſetting at nought, all earthly affaires and delights, in reſpect of Gods will; is heartily in loue with his Word, and continually exerciſing himſelfe, in the ſerious meditating, teaching, and practice therof. For, the word *Ieghe*, which is interpreted to, *meditate*, hath reference, aſwell to the words and workes, as to the thoughts (in which ſence, it is not vſed in the Scriptures only; but the Poet alſo ſaith,—*Meditabor arundine Muſam*.) And it was well expreſſed in the word, *Exerciſe*, in our olde Engliſh Tranſlation.

By the *Law*, is vnderſtood, not onely the morall Lawes; for then, *Bleſſedneſſe* might haue been obtained,

<small>To meditate, what it means
Pſal. 35. 28.
Pſal. 36. 30.</small>

<small>What is ſignified by the Law.</small>

ned, by working, according to the morall vertues, as the heathen *Philo-sophers* taught. Nor, is here meant the Ceremoniall Law alone ; nor that, and the morall together onely. For then, the wicked *Iewes*, though they continued in their vnbeleefe, might become partakers of this happinesse. But the *Law*, in this place (as I told you in my *Preparation to the Psalter*, it was sometime to be vnderstood) signifies the Law of God, as it hath at once, respect to all the ages of the Church, from *Adam*, vntil the end of the world : and therfore comprehends the *Law* of *Grace* also ; yea, all the Doctrine of God, contained in his Word. And this Law, is called the Law of the L O R D ; or if you will haue it, according to the Originalle :

Of יהוה,
the Hebrew
Tetragrammaton, and the
word *Iehovah*. The *Law* of יהוה ; or , I H V H (if we may expresse the Hebrew *Tetragrammaton* in our letters.)

And these Characters, some late Inter-

Interpreters read *Iehouah*; suppofing the forme of that word, to imply as much as ; *He that is, that was, and that is to come.* For, fay they; *Ie,* is a figne of the time to come. *Iueth*; Hee will bee, *Ho*, of the time prefent. *Hoveth*, hee that is. *Vah*, of the time paft. *Havah*, hee was. Which wee will not denie to bee a probable, and ingenious conceite : but indeede, the word *Iehouah*, it felfe; is not confeffed to be fo much as heard of, to be an Hebrew word, among the *Iewes* : neither doth it fignifie any thing in that tongue. Nor can we haue one Teftimony, that the Hebrew *Tetragrammaton* ; was euer anciently fo pronounced. And therefore, vnleffe we had better authority, then probabilities, and vncertaine coniectures, of new Gramarians : I fee no reafon, why we fhould venter, to put this vnknowne name vpon God. Which if it be the right :

Reu. 11. 17.

right: yet, not ſo ſufficiently warranted, to be truely reuealed vnto vs; that we may vſe it, with the ſame confidence, wherewith we pronounce the other names of God. As you may ſee more at large, in the thirteenth Chapter, and third Section of my *preparation to the Pſalter*.

But, to teach vs then, that this *law*; in which it is here ſaid, the bleſſed man delighteth; is not the *law* of man, but of God; know that the vnpronounceable Hebrew word here vſed (and inſteede of which, the Iewes ſpoke *Adonaj*, or *Elohim*; the *Septuagint*, and Apoſtles, Κύριος: the Ancient latine expoſitors, *Dominus*; and the authorized engliſh Tranſlations, for the moſt, LORD) is an eſſentiall and vncommunicable name, of our great, eternall, and euerliuing God; who is moſt truely called, *Hee that is, that was, and that is to come*: and

the firſt Pſalme.

and therefore, whereſoeuer you find this *Tetragrammaton*, יהוה. You may be aſſured, that there is to bee vnderſtood, eyther one, or all the Perſons of the ſacred Trinity. For, whereas the word, *Adonai*, and *Elohim*, are ſometime communicated to others; that is neuer ſo. And therfore, becauſe the word L O R D, by which wee (according to the Apoſtles) haue expreſt it; may be communicable to men: You ſhall vnderſtand; that, whereſoeuer in the laſt Engliſh tranſlation, you finde L O R D, thus in Capitall letters; there, is that glorious, and moſt eſſentiall name of God, to be vnderſtood; which neuer ought to be applied vnto any other.

But (which I had almoſt outſlipt) you muſt note that the holy-Ghoſt, vſeth here the word *Delight*; to ſhew vs further: that the deuotions of a bleſſed man; are not conſtrained, or ſeruile: | The meaning of the word *Delight.*

servile: but rather, proceeding from a true and affectionate pleasure, in the worship of God, with the studie of his word. It must be unto him, as it was to *Dauid: More to be desired then fine Gold; and sweeter then honie, or the honie-combe.* Yea, the excellence of his affection; is further, and another way manifested; in that hee is said to meditate thereon, *Day* and *Night:* For, the *Day* and *Night,* in holy Scripture, hath a three-fold vnderstanding: *Temporall*; *Morall*; and *Allegoricall.* *Temporall,* is the day which wee enioy by the presence of the Sunne: the night thereof, is that which is made by the absence of the same. *Morally,* it is taken for life and death; Prosperitie and aduersity, or such like: and this is also *Metaphoricall. Allegorically,* the old *Law,* is called the Night; and the *Gospell,* tearmed the Day: and therefore *Zacharie* in his song; wherein he spake of

Psal. 19. 10.

Day & Night, what it signifieth.

Gen. 1. 16.

the firſt Pſalme. 61

of Chriſt, and the light reuealed vnto Mankinde in the new Teſtament, faith ; that *The day-ſpring from on high hath viſited vs ; to giue light to them that ſit in darkneſſe.* But Saint *Paul*, writing vnto the *Romanes*, concerning the faith of Chriſt Jeſus ; faith in playner tearmes : *That the Night was paſt, and the Day was at hand.* Euen thus many waies, are the *Day* and *Night* to be vnderſtood, in the booke of God. But in this place ; they are to be conſidered, according to all and euery of theſe. The bleſſed man ; meditateth on the Law of the L O R D, *day* and *night* ; that is : He pondereth all the miſteries of *Ieſus Chriſt* ; as they were promiſed, figured, and propheciced of, in the old *Teſtament*, (which, as the *Night*, ſhadowed them ouer) and then beleeueth and confeſſeth them, as they were fulfilled in the new *Teſtament* ; which was the *Day* that made them ap-

Luke 1. 78. 79.

Rom. 13. 12.

apparant to the whole world: Yea, he is continually enclined vnto the ſtudy of *Piety*, without intermiſſion; Morning and Euening, at Nooneday and at Mid-night; both in Proſperity and Aduerſity; Openly and Secretly. For, many can bee content, perhaps, to ſpare ſome little time in the Day, for the meditation of Gods word: but there are very few, that will breake a ſleepe; and ariſe at night, with *Dauid*, to praiſe God: many can be content, whileſt they gayne any outward benefit, or preferrement by their profeſſion; to be hot and earneſt in the ſtudy thereof: but few dare abide, the blacke and terrible night of perſecution. Nay, a little aduerſity, or worldly inconuenience, cooles all their zeale. Hypocrites by *Day*, that is; openly in the eyes of the world; will be very forward, and ſeeme to be ſtout profeſſors: but, in the *Night*, that is, ſecretly,

the firſt Pſalme.

secretly, and by themselues; where none but God is witnesse: they can laugh at their owne dissembling; and with those people, of whom God speakes by the Prophet *Malachi*, they say thus: *It is in vaine to serue God; and what Profite is it that wee keepe his Commandements?* Againe, there be others, that by *Night*, with *Nicodemus*, dare, peraduenture, come to God; yet by *Day*, are affraid (or ashamed) to be seene in a Religious mans company. But neyther of these, haue well vnderstood what is ment by *Meditating* Gods word *Day* and *Night*: nor are they yet in the way of *Blessednesse*.

Mat. 3. 14.
Ob. 1.

Out of this verse; I doe obserue these things. Firſt, that there is no true happinesse, without the knowledge of God; and the continuall meditation of his word. And that those, who are sincerely adicted to his seruice, and the loue of his *Truth*, are

are in the right way to *Blessednesse*; howsoeuer Atheists, and worldly men, thinke them simple fooles; and their study lost labour.

2. Secondly, I here note; that he cannot promise to himselfe, the reward of *Blessednesse*; that frames a Religion, or way to serue God, out of his owne braine; though neuer so strict, or seeming holy: For, it must not be the Lawes, or traditions of men; that, he must meditate, but the Law of the LORD.

3. Lastly, I doe here learne this Method, for the right study of *Diuinity*; and practise of Christianity. First, that there must be a loue vnto the heauenly word: Secondly, a progresse, or going forward; in the meditation thereof: and lastly, such a constant perseuerance therein, from time to time, and at all times without limitation; in so much, that there must bee some part of euery day and

The first Psalme.

and night, separated for the seruice of God; that we may say with *Dauid*: *Euening, Morning, by Day, and at Midnight, will I pray vnto thee.* | *Psal.* 55. 17.

And, he shall be like a Tree planted, &c: Hauing deliuered in the two former verses, who is a Iust and blessed man, both by the *Negatiue*, and *Affirmatiue*: he now confirmes his former *proposition*: First, by a similitude, taken from a fruitefull Tree, euerlastingly greene: Secondly, by the end, and prosperous successe, of all he takes in hand. By which illustration, we may not imagine, that they are compared with any intent to be made equall *(*For, the blessed estate of a good man, is farre beyond all earthly comparisons*)* But by such knowne things, the holy-Ghost applies his demonstrations to meane capacities. And this kinde of teaching, was vsuall with our *Sauiour*; as appeares by his illustration of Faith; | *Verse* 3.

F

Exercises vpon

Mar. 4. 30.

Mat. 16. 19.
Luke 13. 19.

*Vide Epist.
Henr. Steph.*
before *Mar-
lorets* com-
mentary vpon
the Psalmes.

Faith, and the *kingdome of Heauen*, in likning it vnto a graine of *Mustard-seede*; or comparing Doctrine to Leauen, and such like. Nor hath it beene neglected among prophane writers: For, a liuely Simily, is esteemed among all *Poets* (as well ancient as moderne) to be one of the principall ornaments of their *Poesie*. The Elegancy of whose *Poems*, some haue not beene ashamed to preferre, before these vnimitable *Odes*: whereas, were they as learned in these; as they would seeme to be in the other (at lest, if they could reade them with the same desire and affection) they should here finde; euen, in the literall excellency; as many rare, and admirable expressions. Obserue well this first illustration; and see in what Author you can better it.

For, although men may, for many respects, be resembled vnto Trees; by

The first Pfalme. 67

by reafon of fome fimilitude in their condition (as thus: Euery Tree is eyther for building, or fire wood; and fo, all men are eyther prepared to build up the new *Ierufalem* withall; or, appointed fewell for hell fire) yet; there are certaine choyfe Trees, which doe more properly ferue to figure out the eftate of the Bleffed: as here in this Pfalme, and by this comparifon; you fhall vnderftande. For; hereby, fiue things are made remarkeable in the vpright mans *happineffe*. Firft, he is refembled vnto a Tree that is *planted*. By which, the ftability, and certainty of his eftate is fignified: For, as fuch a Tree; is, where, by the carefulneffe and diligence of fome gardener, or husbandman; he may be manured, and preferued from the choaking of Thornes, and violence of beafts; whilft the wilde Trees of the Forreft, are euer in danger, of fome ruine:

Fiue things obferuable in this illuftration of a godly mans happineffe.

He is Planted.

ine : So, the iuft man, who in the Scripture is refembled vnto a *Palme* tree ; hath this fure and bleffed hope for his comfort : That God, who firft *planted* him ; will alfo protect him from being fpoyled of his leaues by the ftormes of aduerfitie ; or o-uerturned by the malice of the aduerfarie. When it fhall come to paffe, that (as Chrift faid) *Thofe plants which his heauenly Father hath not planted, fhould be rooted vp.*

Moreouer, a Tree *planted* ; infteede of that wilde nature which formerly it retayned ; is bettered, and made more fruitefull by a new plantation : and in like manner ; that man, who had elfe beene naturally apt to bring forth nothing, but the fowre fruits of the flefh ; being planted in the vine-yeard of Gods Church, by the hand of Grace : regenerates, and yeelds forth plentifully, the fweete fruits of the fpirit.

Second-

Pfal. 92.

Math. 15. 13.

Secondly, it is planted by the *Springs, or Riuers of water*; by which, the blessednesse of the Iust man, is further illustrated: For, as that tree, can neither be barren thorough the sterrile drought of the soyle; nor endangered by the scorching heate of Sommer: whose roote is euer moistened, with the nourishing waters of a pleasant streame; So, the regenerate man, hauing his roote in Christ (where the euer springing fountaines of his Grace; with sweete dewes of mercy, continually cherish it) euen he, shall alway flourish. For, neither can he be consumed as the wicked are, by the burning fire of Gods indignation; nor made vnprofitable for want of nourishment. To the same effect speakes the Prophet *Ieremy*, in his illustration of such a mans happinesse; by a similitude taken from the like Tree. *He shall bee* (saith he) *as a Tree that is planted by the*

Secondly, he is placed by the Riuers of water.

Ierem. 17. 18.

F 3

the waters; and that spreadeth forth her rootes by the Riuer, and shall not see when heate commeth: but her leafe shall be greene, and shall not be carefull in the yeere of drouth, neither shall cease from yeelding fruite. By the *Riuers of water*, in this *Psalme*, is Allegorically meant; the word of God, and his Sacraments: which, are the means whereby he infuseth into vs, the graces of his Spirit; keepes vs growing in Faith; and nourisheth fruits, to eternall life.

Thirdly, it *giueth fruite in due season*: Whereby is manifested another propertie of the blessed Iustman: *By the fruite* (faith our Sauiour) *the Tree is knowne*: and so is the iust man by his workes: Who, in bringing forth his spirituall fruits, may (not vnfitly) be resembled to a Tree. For, as the Tree brings forth fruits for others, rather then for it selfe: So, the vpright man fructifies

---

Sidenotes:
- The Riuers of waters, what they meane.
- Thirdly, he is fruitfull, and that in season.

the firſt Pſalme.

fies, and ſends forth good workes, and deedes of Charitie; not, thereby to merit ought for himſelfe; but to glorifie God, and to benefit others. Which is a noble *Bleſſedneſſe.* For, as the Apoſtle ſaith; *it is a more bleſ-ſed thing to giue, then to receiue.* Further; we haue the Pronoune *His:* to ſhew vs, that as the Tree giueth forth no fruite but his owne, and according to his kinde; So, the *righteous*, doth the workes proper to a regenerate man; all the good deedes which he performeth, are done with that which is his owne: and ſo cherefully; that they may be called *His.* Yea, he yeeldeth forth good fruits, according to the meaſure, and qualitie of thoſe gifts which he hath receiued. Laſtly, the Tree giueth forth her fruite *in ſeaſon,* or in time: that is; in her time of fruitfulneſſe; and ſo; the vpright man, doth good in due time; euen vpon the

Acts. 20.

The pronoun *His.*

When, fruit is giuen in ſeaſon, or in time

F 4 firſt

firſt occaſion offered. He is neuer barren, when neceſſity requires fruit. If in one day, a thouſand men neede his comforting hand; he is euer willing, according to his ability, to giue redreſſe vnto them all. Neyther too ſoone, nor too late comes his charity: but, like ſweete and well ripened fruite, is euer, then ready to be receiued; when it may be moſt acceptable to God, timely, in reſpect of himſelfe; and very profitable to others.

Fruit, what it ſignifieth.

But indeede, by the *fruit* here is principally meant Faith, and the confeſſion of ſaluation by Chriſt: which can neuer be, without workes. And that is it, which our *Saviour meant*, when hee ſaid: *Herein is my Father glorified, that you beare much fruit.*

Ioh. 15. 8.

Fourthly He is euer flouriſhing.

Fourthly, *His leafe ſhall not fade:* Yet; the ſimilitude holds very properly, in that the *bleſſed* man is reſembled vnto a tree, not onely fruitfull, but flouriſhing alſo; and euer adorned

the firſt Pſalme.

dorned with the comely ornament of greene leaues. For, as the *Palme-tree*, whereto the Iuſt man is likened, in the 92 *Pſalme* (and from which tree, it is very likely, this ſimilitude was taken) is neuer, as *Pliny* faith, without fruit ; and therefore muſt, confequently, bee alwayes greene : ſo, the Iuſt man is continually beautified, with all the accompliſhments of a Chriſtian ; full of holy thoughts, plentifull in profitable words, and ſeriouſly exerciſed in good actions, without wearineſſe in well-doing : and to accompany that fruitfulneſſe, enioyeth ſuch a perpetuall happines, as growes at no time ſubiect to any momentary change. What ſtorm ſoeuer happens, hee is ſtill in a flouriſhing and profperous eſtate : yea, when the vngodly (like thoſe trees which are altered, according to the difpoſition of euery ſeaſon) muſt loſe, in the winter of their triall, all that

Plin. lib. 16. *cap.* 20.

Exercises vpon

that vncertaine glory, gotten in the spring-time of their prosperity: euen then; the happinesse of the righteous is so permanent, as the coldest frost of aduersity, can neuer strip him of his faire leaues: that is: no persecution shall bee able to take from him, the faire liuery of his profession, nor put him, beside the Crowne of an immortall glory.

5. What euer hee doth, prospers.

Fiftly, *whatsoeuer he doth, shall prosper*: In these words, hee doth (as it were) summe vp, and make perfect his expression of *happinesse*. And the *Prophet* doth it without the *Metaphor*; for, I haue obserued, that to expresse one and the same sentence; partly by the figure, and partly without: is ordinary in the *Psalmes*. Yet, the great Scholler, and Cardinall, *Bellarmine*; in his Comment vpon this *Psalme*, would haue these words (*whatsoeuer hee doth shall prosper*) to be referred vnto the *Tree*. Then, hauing

the first Psalme.

uing interpreted the Hebrew Verbe, *Iasliach*; *prosperare faciet*, will make to prosper: he gathers from thence, an actiue vertue to be in the tree; helping on the ripening of his owne fruits. And, by the application of the similitude, would also note vnto vs; that, there were an actiue vertue of *free will* in man, concurring with the Diuine grace, to meritorious works. But, by his leaue, it seemes to mee, not so to bee vnderstood; for, that interpretation, is both harsh in the sence, and contradictory to the opinion of most Expositors. Yea, one of his owne faction, *Lorinus*, a learned *Iesuite*, writing on this *Psalme*, sayth; that it ought rather to be vnderstood of the *Iust man*, then of the Tree. *Lyra*, a very ancient Expositor, hath so taken it also: and so haue the greatest number of most authenticall Writers. For which cause; I rather allow it: but especially, by reason

Exerci∫es vpon

∫on I beleeue it, to be indeed the be∫t, and natural fence of this Text; agreeable to the happy e∫tate of a good man; and the ∫ame ble∫∫ing, which the *Scriptures* te∫tifie, to haue beene vouch∫afed to ∫uch as feare God. For, it is ∫ayd of *Io∫eph*: *The* LORD *made all that he did, to pro∫per in his hands.*

Gene∫. 39.

A Caueat.

But from hence, wee mu∫t neither gather, that all tho∫e are good men, who pro∫per, and thriue, in the things of this life; neither imagine, it is heere promi∫ed, that the Righteous ∫hall bee without troubles, or hinderances, in their temporall affaires. The meaning rather is: that al things, (euen tho∫e) wherein they ∫eeme to the world mo∫t mi∫erable, ∫hould redound to their comfort; and pro∫per them in the way to eternall life. According to the ∫aying of S. *Paul*; *All things worke together for good, to them that loue God.* *Dauid* al∫o confirmeth

Rom. 8. 28.

The first Psalme.

firmeth the same, out of his owne experience: for, saith he; *It was good for mee, that I was in trouble.* And indeede, it is the end which crownes all, and that which makes the vndertaking prosperous, or vnfortunate: not the occurrences, that happen well, or ill, in the procceding. For, though a *Commander* in the warres finde, that all his determinations proceeded ill, in the ordering of his Battles; and that all his *Stratagems*, turned a while, to his hinderance: yea, though with the losse, of many thousands of his men, and the effusion of much of his owne bloud, he hath endured a terrible, and sharp encounter. Yet, if at last, the victory bee on his side, he hath his aime; and thinks, that his vndertaking prospered in his hands. So, though a Christian man hath, in this life, suffered innumerable miseries; though matters haue succeeded so ill with him, that sorrow

row vpon sorrow, and mischeefe vpon mischeefe, ouerwhelmed him, and euery thing that he endeauoured, fell out contrary to his expectation; yet, if at laſt (as queſtionleſſe he ſhall) he reape the Crowne of immortall glory: we may very well ſay, that *whatſoeuer he did, hath proſpered*. Yea, his miſeries and infirmities, were for his good, ſuffered to come vpon him; euen they alſo, proſpred in his hands; and were the meanes to make him, a right bleſſed man.

Bleſſedneſſe, two-fold. Luke 14. 15.

For, you muſt vnderſtand, that there is a two-fold *Bleſſedneſſe*; *Beatitudo in via, & in Regno*; A bleſſedneſſe in the *way*, and in the *Kingdom*. That in the *way*, is alſo two-fold; one, on the right hand; and the other, on the left: The *left-hand* happineſſe; is the abundance of temporall proſperities. For, the *Pſalmiſt* hauing reckoned vp many temporall benefits; concludeth with theſe words.

the first Psalme.

words. *Blessed are the people, that bee so. Happinesse* on the *right hand*, is the gift of spirituall graces, bestowed in this life. For, saith our Sauiour, *Blessed are the poore in spirit, the humble; those that hunger and thirst after righteousnesse,* &c. But the last of these *blessings*; appertaines onely to the children of God: the other, are indifferently bestowed, both on good and bad. *Psal.* 144. 15.

Matth. 5.

The *Blessednesse* in the *Kingdome*; is that, which is principally meant in this *Psalme*: and indeede, the most perfect compleat happinesse. The possession of that, wee haue now in hope onely. None, but the sonnes of God, can enioy it, in the other world (as is aforesayd) nor, can any man, but those that haue their hearts enlarged, by the Holy Ghost; enter into a worthy thought thereof, here. For, as S. *Paul* saith; *It is that, which eye hath not seene, nor eare* 1 *Cor.* 2. 9.

care heard, neither comes it into the heart of man, to conceiue what God hath prepared for them, that loue him. It is fo many degrees, beyond the felicity of this life, that the moſt bleſſed man is miſerable here, in compariſon of the happineſſe, which hee ſhall bee crowned with all, after his death. And therfore, if you haue reſpect to that, which may moſt properly bee called *Bleſſedneſſe*, it muſt bee loked for in another world ; for, as the *Poet* faith :

———— *Diciq́. beatus*
Ante obitum nemo, fupremaq́. fu-
nera debet.

We none may bleſſed call,
Before their funerall.

<small>What makes perfect Bleſ-ſedneſſe.</small> But, becauſe carnall men, are too too much perſwaded, that true felicity may bee enioyed in this life ; I would

the firſt Pſalme.

would haue them learne, what is required, to the making vp of a perfect *Bleſſedneſſe*. For, they muſt know, there are three things, which are of the eſſence of true felicity. The firſt is, the knowledge of the *Cheefe Good*; *Ioh.* 17. 13. *this is eternal life, to know the only true God, and him whom thou haſt ſent, Ieſus Chriſt*, faith S. *Iohn*. Secondly, there muſt be a fruition, and full enioying of that *Cheefe Good*, being ſo knowne. And laſtly, a perfect delight, and contentation in that which is enioyed. Without euery of which circumſtances, there is no perfect happineſſe. For, hee that enioyes, and is contented; without the full knowledge, of the certainty, and worth of that, which he enioyes: hath but a dull vncertaine contentation; and is depriued of a great part of his felicity.

In like manner, hee that knowes what it is to bee happy, and hath it

G   not

not in poſſeſſion, is ſo farre from happineſſe; that he is the more miſerable, by the apprehenſion which he hath, of the great good hee wanteth. But if hee did know, and enioy to; yet, if hee had not the bleſſing of a contented minde, it were as much, as if he enioyed nothing.

Cap. 3.   S. *Auguſtine* hath a ſpeech, much to this purpoſe, in his firſt Booke, *De Moribus Eccleſiæ Catholicæ*: For, ſaith he, *Beatus neque ille (quantum exiſtimo) dici poteſt, qui non habet quod amat qualecunq́ ſit; neq́ qui habet quod amat, ſi noxium ſit; neq. qui non amat quod habet, etiamſi optimum ſit.* That is: *Neither, as I thinke, can hee bee ſayd, to be bleſſed, who enioyeth not what hee loueth, whatſoeuer it be; nor hee, that attaineth to what hee affecteth, if it bee hurtfull; nor hee, that is not pleaſed with that, which he poſſeſſeth, although it bee the beſt thing.* And hee giueth this reaſon: *Nam, & qui appetit quod adipiſci*

the firſt Pſalme.

adipiſci non poteſt cruciatur ; & qui adeptus eſt, quod appetendum non eſt, fallitur ; & qui non appetit quod adipiſcendum eſſet ; ægrotat. Id eſt: *For hee which deſireth what cannot be attained, is vexed* ; *hee that hath attained vnto that, which proues not worthy deſiring, is deceiued* ; *and hee which affecteth not, what is indeede worthy the enioying, is ſicke* ; *or faulty in himſelf.* And ſo, not one of theſe, can bee bleſſed: becauſe, neither of their ſoules is without vexation and miſery. For, if it might bee ſo ; theſe two contraries, *Bleſſednesse*, and *Vnhappineſſe* ; ſhould dwell together at the ſame time, in one man : which were impoſſible.

This *Bleſſednesse*, cannot then, conſiſt in temporall & tranſitory things. For, though we may haue the knowledge of their vtmoſt good, & get alſo the poſſeſſion of them ; yet, it is impoſſible, they ſhould giue vs a content,

True bleſſedneſſe conſiſteth not in temporall things.

G 2

tent, beyond which, nothing is to be defired. For, the foule of man, is of a fpirituall nature; and of fo large an apprehenfion, that the whole world is not able to fill it. Though you fhould feede the boundleffe defire of man, with Kingdome vpon Kingdome; hee would neuer finde end of defiring, vntill hee had the poffeffion of the whole world, with all the creatures therein: and though he could compaffe that: yet, becaufe the mortalitie of his body, would euer put him in feare, to be depriued therof; he would neuertheleffe be full of difquiet. Nay, were it poffible, that feare, might be taken away alfo: it would then difcontent him, that there were not more worlds, & new things, to couet and poffeffe. And fo, he would bee vnhappy, in the middeft of all that happineffe.

Ecclef. 1. 17. This, made *Soloman* fay (when he had fearched into the nature of all creatures,

The first Psalme.

creatures, and fought to pleafe his foule, in whatfoeuer it longed for) that all things vnder the Sunne (euen knowledge, and thofe which are accounted the beft) were vanity, and vexation of fpirit. And this, if worldly men did better confider, doubtleffe, they would not fo much adict themfelues to the things of this life: but feeke to haue their foules, rather filled with the knowledge of God; who is only able to fatisfie them, & without whom, they are euer empty, and feeking vp and downe for that, which fhould fill them. For, the end to which God created the foule of man, was (as *S. Auguftine* faith) That fhe might know him; in knowing, loue him; and in louing, enioy him: wherein confifteth perfect *bleffedneffe*, neuer to be loft againe; and that, which is principally meant in this *Pfalme*.

The *Doctrines*, that we may gather from

Exercises vpon

from this third verfe, are thefe.

Doct. 1.   Firft, that if the *Bleſſed* are planted, & not as naturally growing trees: then, the efficient caufe of our faluation, is God. For, it is of his gracious fauour, that we are planted in the Vineyard of his Church; otherwife, wee had beene, as wilde Olivetrees, growing on the barren mountaines.

Doct. 2.   Secondly, in that it is fayd. The Bleſſed is as the Tree, planted *by the riuers of waters:* Wee are taught, what the inftrumentall caufes of our faluatiō are; euen the Word of God & his bleſſed Sacraments. For, by the *Springs*, or *Riuers of waters*, are thofe allegorically vnderftood (as I fayd before) & in that, they are fayd to be planted; thereby, wee alfo gather further, that fuch as are out of the Church, till they bee there feated, by the fountaines of (life and inoculated into the myfticall body of *Chriſt*) are

What the Riuers of waters fignifie.

the firſt Pſalme.

are not yet in the ſtate of *Bleſſed-neſſe*.

Thirdly, wee may hereby know, whether wee belong to God, or no. For, if wee bee trees of his Vineyard, wee cannot but bee ſenſible, of the ſweet graces and operations of his Spirit : and ſhall not be found barren, of thoſe ſpirituall fruits, which God wil looke for, in their due time. And be aſſured, that if wee bee vnprofitable ; though wee carry neuer ſo many faire leaues of hypocriſie, to couer our ſterility : we ſhal one day bee ſtript of them, and caſt into the fire.

Fourthly and laſtly, wee are here taught, not to iudge of men, by their proſperity, or aduerſity ; but, howſoeuer their outward affaires ſucceede, to eſteeme them bleſſed, and happy men, that loue and honour God. And ſo, I conclude this firſt part of the *Pſalme*, which doth in breefe deliuer thus much : *That hee,*

Doct. 3.

Doct. 4.

Exerciſes vpon

which would be a bleſſed man, ought to auoyd all manner of ſinne, loue Gods Word: meditate it, practiſe it, goe forward in that practiſe, bring forth fruits of righteouſneſſe; and continue vnto the end of his life, in that courſe.

The

The second part of the PSALME.

4. **T**He vngodly are not so: but are like the Chaffe, which the winde driueth away.

5. Therefore the vngodly shall not stand in the iudgement, nor sinners in the Congregation of the righteous.

6. For, the LORD knoweth the way of the righteous: but the way of the vngodly shall perish.

The

Ver. 4.

THe Prophet; or, rather the Holy-Ghoſt, by the mouth of the Prophet, hauing in the former part of this Pſalme; in an excellent manner, ſet downe vnto vs the bleſſed eſtate of a good Chriſtian; and in diuers particulars diſcouered, and illuſtrated his matchleſſe *Bleſſedneſſe*; that we might be thereby drawne to loue and ſeeke it. Doth now, in this other part, briefly (yet as fully) acquaint vs with the miſerable condition of the vnbeleeuing ſinner. euen in theſe few words: *The vngodly are not ſo*. For, they carrie in them a direct *Antitheſis* vnto the whole firſt part of the *Pſalme*; and imply euery whit aſmuch, as if the Prophet had ſaid: *The wicked are ſuch*; as neyther diſcontinue their *walke*, in the *Counſels* of the *vngodly*: nor ſhunne the *way* of *euill doers*; nor auoide the *ſeate* of the *ſcornefull*. And therefore, are in no poſſibility, to be

ſo

The first Pfalme.

so happy as are the righteous. And this the *Septuagint*, very powerfully expresseth, by doubling the Negatiue, οὐκ οὕτως οἱ ἀσεβεῖς, οὐκ οὕτως, *the wicked are nor so, nor so*. To wit: nor so holy in their life; nor so bleffed in their end. They are not so ftudious of Gods word, as the righteous; and therefore he taketh no such knowledge of their waies: they doe not so affect the *way* of his feruice; & therefore he fuffers their *way* to perifh: they are not so *planted*; and therefore not so safe, but in danger to be rooted vp, by the iudgements of God: they are not so fituated, where they may be nourifhed, by the moyfture of the *Riuers* of Gods grace, conueyed by his word and Sacraments, into their hearts; and therefore, not so flourifhing; but in danger to be withered by the burning heate of his Indignation: they are not so fruitfull; and therefore, likely to vndergoe a curse, with

The diffimilitude that is betweene the wicked, and the righteous.

with the barren fig-Tree. They are in nothing anfwerable to the condition of the well planted Tree, here fpoken of: but vngodly men, and Hypocrites, for the moft part, yeeld no fruit at all. If they bring forth any; it is not good. And then it is no better then if they were vnfruitfull: *For euery Tree that bringeth not forth good fruite, fhall be hewen downe, and caft into the fire.* Or though it might, perhaps, for fome refpects, be called good fruite, which they giue; then it is none of their owne : For, they doe, like moft of the great rich men in thefe dayes; who, other while indeede, relieue a few poore foules. But it is with the fruit of other mens labours. Yea, they leaue many goodly fhewes of Charity behinde them; with that which had beene, with extreme couetoufneffe and oppreffion, torne, as it were, out of the throates of their poore Neighbours.

Math. 3. 10.

the firſt Pſalme.

bours. Or if we ſhould grant that it was their owne fruite they gaue ; yet, it would be found to come out of ſeaſon, and when there is no great neede of it: whereas a cup of cold water ; giuen vnto a poore man in extremity : comes in better ſeaſon, then a great deale of vaine liberality at other times. But, if wee ſhould yeeld them this ; that their fruite came in *ſeaſon* ; it is in their owne *ſeaſon* then : And when is that ? Forſooth, now and then ; perhaps at ſuch times, when as the cuſtomes of their Countrie require publike hoſpitality. And then ; it is but forc't, ſowre, and unſauorie fruite. For, moſt commonly, for one honeſt man that ſhall ſatisfie his neceſſity among them ; two Ruffians ſhall be made drunke. Or elſe their *ſeaſon* is, when they may take occaſion to make moſt ſhew to the world, of the ſeeming good they doe : like the *Phariſies*,

The Worldlings ſeaſon in which hee brings fruite.

sies, that blew Trumpets, when they gaue almes. But indeede, the principall time and seafon of their vintage is; when the Axe is set vnto the roote of the Tree. Then; when the leaues of their youth, and prosperity are fallen off; the branches quite withered; the bodie rotten, ready to ſtinke with putrifaction; and they in caſe no more to hoard vp, or keepe it vnto themſelues; then (if the *Diuell* doe not come before they be aware, and carry them away by the Rootes; as ſometime he ſerueth old Trees in the Forreſt) it may ſo fall out, that they leaue a few vnſeaſonable fruits behind them: which often, in fine painted Almeſhouſes; make ſhew of more reliefe, then is halfe performed.

Nor are the vngodly, in reſpect of their vnfruitfulneſſe, or vntimelineſſe in bearing fruite (onely) ſo contrary to the righteous: but euen their leaues,

Math. 6. 2.

the first Psalme.

leaues, those their faire leaues; that make them seeme so flourishing, are but the Sommer ornaments of prosperity; and must wither and fall off, in the winter of their triall. Yea, nothing they take in hand shall prosper them in the way to true happinesse; therefore all their vndertakings are in vaine. And as the holy-Ghost here saith: *It is nothing so with them*, as with the Godly.

Thus; exceeding elegantly, hath the Prophet described the misery of the wicked, by opposing it vnto the felicitie of the Iust. Which he yet maketh more apparant: and, howsoeuer the world esteemes her owne as fortunate men; he shewes the contrary. Seeming also, not contented to set it forth by a similitude, directly contrarie to the former; he leaueth the first Metaphor, and resembles them, to the vilest and lightest *Chaffe*: as if else, he should not haue

Exerciſes vpon

Why the wicked are reſembled to Chaffe.

haue made them contemptible enough, in his expreſſion.

And here I could ſhew, how properly the wicked may, for diuerſe reaſons, be likened unto *Chaffe*. As in regard of that lightneſſe, which makes them inconſtantly carried away, with euery vanity: or in reſpect of their ſterility, with ſuch like. Which (becauſe euery reaſonable capacity can apprehend them) I will omit: & only deſire you to take from hence this obſeruation. To wit, that the enemies, and oppreſſors of Gods Children; with all other vngodly men (though they be admired of the world, and ſeeme mighty and vnmouable in their owne haughty opinions) are, (neuertheles indeed) poore baſe things; meere *Chaffe*. Nay, the worſt and lighteſt of it: euen that which is ſcattered euery way with the winde. Or worſe, if worſe may be: For, they are not onely vn-

the firſt Pſalme.

vnſetled, and reſtleſly driuen too and fro, in their owne vaine practiſes; or tumbled vp and downe by the diſtempered furie of their miſerable affections: but their riches, honours, powers, and *their very place of being* (as *Dauid* faith) *ſhall decay, and be no more found.* For, the terrible winde of Gods wrath, ſhall puffe all, into euerlaſting perdition. Yea, Gods iudgement will ruſh vpon them on a ſuddaine, and inuiſibly, as a wind: which ſhall come they know not from whence; and carrie them they know not whether. Nor ſhall their ſtrength, eminence, or greatneſſe, defend them. But, as the winde makes moſt hauock among tall Cedars, on high Mountaines: So, ſhall their pride and loftineſſe, make them more ſubiect to the tempeſt of Gods indignation. As appeared in *Pharaoh, Nebuchadonezor, Herod*; and ſuch other. But ſome may

H   ſay

fay; many vngodly men liue free from all thofe miferies and croffes here fpoken off. Truely, it feemes fo for a time ; but the greater will be their forrow at the laft. Nay, I am perfwaded, that euen in this life, and at the beft; they haue fo much bitternefe, to make vnfauorie all their delights : as, if we could look into the hearts and confciences, of thofe that feeme happieft men to the worldward. I beleeue we fhould difcouer fo much horror, and difquietneffe ; as would make vs fet light by our difcontentments. For, many of them, amid their aboundance of wealth and honours ; are more diftempered with toyes ; then a conftant Chriftian is, with his greateft afflictions. And if trifles will not moue them ; they haue matters of greater confequence to difturbe their reft. One grieues, to fee the familie, which he thought to make honourable, by his

The vnhappynes of worldly men in this life.

The first Psalme.

his owne pollicy; quite rooted out by the improuidence of his Children: Yea, the miserable Catiue, liues to behold his sonnes prodigalitie, consume his vsury; and yet hath not the power to afford himselfe the benefit of his owne labours, neither to doe one good deede, that may purchase a prayer for him; untill it is too late. Another, hath labour'd for the applause of the people; and with vexation of spirit, comes to heare his name made the iust subiect of Libels; and himselfe reputed odious in the common-wealth. One, is sicke, for some disgrace receiued from his Prince. A second, grieued with the vnkindenes of those whom he thought his best friends. A third, mad at the pride of his equall. A fourth, ready to hang himselfe for the insolence of his inferiour. A fift, pines with enuying at his superiour. A sixt, sleepes not for desire of preferment.

ferment. A seauenth, trembles through feare of losing his office. The eighth, hath a wife that is more shame, and discontent vnto him, then all these. And, which is worse then that too; he knowes not what shall become of him at last. For, sometime he thinkes that men die like beasts, without hope of another life. And then, it grieues him, that he must for euer, leaue the world, which he so much loued. Another while, he remembers he hath heard of a *God*; and *a Day of Iudgement*. Which, putteth him into such a desperat feare; that he is neuer alone, but his heart quakes; and his guilty Conscience so stings & threatens him, with hell and damnation; that hee sometime wisheth hee were indeede, realy *dust*, or *Chaffe*; and that, the winde might scatter him into nothing.

Oh God! that I were able so to serue this

the first Psalme.

this, into the hearts of worldlings; as to make their muddy apprehensions, more sensible of their vnhappinesse: and allure them, to seeke for that true and perfect felicitie, which is here promised. But alas! it is beyond my power. For the whole world (almost) hath runne through all the degrees of wickednesse; and the greatest part, are become Benchers, in that damnable society of Scorners: with whom, it is impossible to preuaile. Nay, my God; would thou mightst bee pleased (though it were but so farre, to enable mee with thy spirit) that the apprehension of these things, might euer continue in my selfe, so feruent, as at sometimes they be. For, by that meanes, I should not onely; neuer more againe, be carried away by those vanities and infirmities, whereunto youth and the frailty of my condition is prone; but become also, so highly delighted with the contemplation, and hope *of that incomparable bleſſedneſſe which is prepared for the louers of thy Law: that the worlds minions ſhold ſee, I did not meerely in word; but truely in deede; neglect, and deſpiſe all thoſe things, which they account either felicities, or diſaſters in this life. Yea, they ſhould perceiue me, ſo farre from thinking my ſelfe a miſerable man; For being in pouerty, ſlandered, neglected, contemned, tortured with ſuch like: or, from imagining my ſelfe a happy man, in the fruition of that vaine fauour, honour, wealth, eaſe, fame, and reſpect, which they glorie in: as, they ſhould with enuie be forced to confeſſe within themſelues; that, by a meanes which the world knew not, I had ariued at ſuch felicitie; as in reſpect thereof, their happineſſe, was but as dirt, and dung to Gold and Siluer. And perhaps alſo when they were in their greateſt earthly pompe: It ſhould more vexe them, to behold me (whom they account miſerable)*

ble) *disdayning those things as triuiall, wherein they place their highest blessednesse*; then it can delight, or content them, to possesse those pleasures or preferments which they enioy. This, oh Lord were possible; if thou wouldst alwaies preserue in thy seruant, the consideration, which at sometime thou vouchsafest to bestow vpon me. But I am the meanest of thy children; and I confesse that these good affections, and apprehensions, which I sometime haue of the blessednesse here promised: doe often; yea, too often faile in me. And then, I doe not onely shrinke as much as any other, vnder the burthen of temporall afflictions: but my heart is also intangled, with those desires, and preposterous contentments, that vainest world-lings seeke after. Which weakenesse; I both heartily pray thee (Oh God) to heale in me; and surely beleeue also, that thou wilt doe it, when it shall be most for thy glory, and my furtherance, in the way *of trueſt* Bleſſedneſſe. *The thought whereof; hath now ſo highly tranſported me; that, I had almoſt forgotten what I had more to ſay, touching the infelicity of the wicked.* But now I deſcend againe, to ſpeake of them.

Therefore the vngodly ſhall not ſtand in the Iudgement, &c. You haue formerly beene giuen to vnderſtand, of the great difference, that is betweene the *Righteous* and the *vngodly*; both in their condition, and their reward. Now, he ſhewes that a difference will be betwixt them ; not in this life only : but alſo in the laſt day. For, that is the principal *Iudgement* here ment : and ſpoken of, *per Antonomaſiam*, as the *Arabick* Interpreter, by theſe words, *in fine*, doth plainely denote.

They ſhall not be able to ſtand in the iudgment, nor in the congregation of the righteous.

That is ; they ſhall not be approued but haue iudgement pronounced againſt

Verſe. 5.

To ſtand, what it ſignifies.

the firſt Pſalme. 105

againſt them, to their ouerthrow, at the generall *Doome*. For, ſo are theſe words, *ſhall not ſtand*, to bee vnderſtood. And the phraſe is not onely proper to the *Hebrewes*; but vſuall among the *Latines*, and vs alſo. *Cicero* hath, *Cauſa cadere*; which, is after the ſame manner of ſpeaking: And *Terence*, where hee ſaith, *Se, vix ſictiſſe*; meanes that ſome of his Fables were ſcarſe approued of, by the common people. And when, with vs, a man comes to his triall, before a Iudge: we often ſay, *Hee cannot ſtand out*. Or, that, *Hee will haue a fall*; when we meane, his cauſe ſhall not receiue approbation.

Now, the reaſon, why *the vngodly ſhall not ſtand in Iudgement*, &c. is partly ſhewn in the former verſe. And that is, becauſe they are but as the *Chaffe*; euen the refuſe of man-kind, vaine, light, vnneceſſary perſons, without fruit, wholly ly voyd of that worth and weight, which fhould make them of efteeme in the fight of God. Yea, fuch as cannot bee able to endure his iudgements; becaufe, they will bee vnto them, *as the winde, fcattering Chaffe.* Alas! who would imagine this (feeing the brauery of this worlds Fauorites) but that the Spirit of God hath fayd it? Now, they are fo mighty, that they thinke it impoffible, to bee mooued. They haue *Counfells*, in which the *Righteous* are not to *walke: Wayes*, wherein they muft not *ftand: Iudgements*, in which the innocent dare not appeare: And they haue Affemblies, and folemne meetings, from which they exclude all good men. But, when the Iudgement here fpoken of, comes (for there will come fuch a day) the poore difperfed, and defpifed members of *Chrift*, fhall bee gathered into one *Congregation*, whereinto no vncleane thing

thing ſhall enter. Nor, ſhall the vngodly mingle among them, in their Aſſembly; but bee ſeparated from them, and thruſt vnto the left hand of the Iudge. And although, here they may appeare powerfull; make great boaſt of their authority; and, perhaps, in our Courts of Iudgement on earth, be able to ſtand out, vntill they haue ruined the innocent (for, in any cauſe, fauours are to bee had, among the corrupted Iudges of this world.) Yet, in the generall *Doome*, when euery man ſhall appeare naked, without bribes; and before a Iudge, that can neuer be corrupted. Alas! what will thoſe things? thoſe vain things, profit them, wherin they now glory? Then, thoſe noble Tyrants ſhall be glad, to ſneake into corners, and cranies of the earth, to hide themſelues from the preſence of God. They ſhall not haue power, to ſtand among thoſe poore men, o-
uer

108 | *Exercises vpon*

uer whom they haue heretofore tyrannized; nor bee able to abide the leaſt triall of Gods Iuſtice: but, affrighted with the terrible afpect of their angry Iudge, and tortured with the horrours of an accufing confcience; ſhall be vtterly amazed, deiected, confounded, and with a diſtracted feare, be glad (& in vain be glad) to intreat the hills, that they would fall down, and couer them. That you may be confident, of the terror of this Iudgement; & that, there will be a feparation of the wicked, from the Congregation of the righteous (as it is here fayd) See, what our Sauiour ſpeaketh, in the 25 chapter of Saint *Matthewes* Gofpell, to this purpofe.

Matth. 25.

What Iudgement the Holy Ghoſt meaneth in this Pfalm.

But, this place may haue refpect to other *Iudgements*. For, befide that great and generall *Doome*; there is a two-fold Iudgement, in this life: wherein the *wicked ſhall not bee able to ſtand*. One is, the *Iudgement* of themfelues,

the firſt Pſalme.

ſelues; when their owne conſcience ſhall accuſe; and condemning them as guilty, caſt them downe headlong into deſpaire. The other is, when the plagues and iudgements of God are ſuffered, to lay hold of them in this world, for the example of others. Now, in neither of theſe; ſhall they be able to ſtand out before God.

Note here, that thoſe Hebrew words, which are interpreted in our Tranſlation, *They ſhall not ſtand*, are in the *Septuagint*, and vulgar Latine Taanſlations, turned thus, οὐκ ἀναϛήσουῒ, *Non reſurgunt*, that is, *They riſe not againe*. And thence, ſome haue weakly and ignorantly gathered, that the wicked ſhall not riſe in the fleſh, to come and receiue Iudgement in the laſt Day. Yea, with this opinion, was that learned Father, *Origen*, a while deluded. But, it is a great hereſie: for, they ſhall ſurely bee raiſed, and ſummoned
to

to that Doome (as appeareth in many places of holy Scripture) but there indeed, they fhal not be able to ftand out in their owne Iuftification, as belonging to the Affembly of the righteous. Becaufe, when they fhall thinke, to excufe themfelues; the King fhall turne them forth, with this terrible fentence. *Goe, yee curfed, into euerlafting fire, which is prepared for the Deuill and his Angells.*

Matth. 25. 41.

Obfer. Hence then I obferue; that there fhall bee a generall Doome, wherein both good and bad fhall be fummoned, before the Tribunall Seat of God. And that, althogh Hypocrites, like tares amongft wheat (or rather, like good wheat) may be fuffered, in this life, to fhrowd themfelues in the Church of God, and come into the Congregation of the Righteous, vnder the name of *Chriftians*: yet, in the harueft (that is) in this *Iudgment*; hee wlll feperate them. And the vngodly

the firſt Pſalme.

godly ſhall not be able to *ſtand*, in that Aſſembly of the Iuſt; but *The Lord will gather the Righteous, which are the wheat; into his Granard : & caſt the ſinners, which are the chaffe ; into vnquenchable fire.*   *Matth.* 13. 14.

But, that no weake conſcience may be driuen into deſpaire. I deſire the Reader, not to imagine, that euery man, who hath the pollutions of ſin, is in danger of this ſeparation ; for, euery man is ſo guilty of ſinne, that if God ſhould marke all that were a-miſſe, and enter into Iudgements with his ſeruants *:* None were able to *ſtand in the Iudgement.* No, not the moſt Righteous ; neither ſhould any fleſh be ſaued in his ſight. We muſt then conſider, that there be two ſorts of *Sinners.* The one regenerate, who offends vnwillingly ; and falling into tranſgreſſions, through infirmity, by repentance, true contrition, and amendment of life, riſeth againe ; and

A Caueat.

Two ſorts of ſinnes.

and seekes forgiuenesse, in his Redeemer, *Iesus Christ*. The other, vnregenerate; who, out of wicked impiety, and malicious wilfullnesse, followes without repentance, the study and practice of sinne; obstinately refusing, or neglecting the grace of *Christ*, And they are such, whose estate is so miserable, to be excluded, from the *Assembly of the Righteous*. The other, laying hold on *Christ*, are by faith made righteous in him, and shall be reckoned among the faithfull and happy Congregation.

Ver. 6. *For, the* LORD *knoweth the way of the righteous*, &c. The reason is here giuen, why the Iust man is so much more happy, then the Sinner; and how it comes to passe, that, *hee walketh not in the Counsells of the vngodly, nor standeth in the way of sinners, nor sitteth in the seat of the scornefull*. And why, in the last Iudgement,

The firſt Pſalme.

ment, there ſhall bee a ſeparation made, and a difference put betweene the good and the bad. And it is this, *God knoweth the way of the righteous. and the way of the vngodly ſhall periſh.* Which implies, that there is a contrariety in their *way*; and that therfore, they cannot meet in one Congregation.

But why is it ſayd, *God knowes the way of the Righteous?* Doth hee not alſo know the way of the wicked, you will ſay? I anſwer, yes. For, Gods diuine knowledge extends it ſelfe to all. Yet, in this place, the word, *knoweth*, includes, eſpecially, a regard, or approbation; and is, as if he ſhould haue ſayd, God *acknowledgeth, takes care of, regards,* or *alloweth* the way of the Righteous: and, becauſe their endeauours and aimes are, to ſhunne the Counſels of the vngodly, and by obedient directing themſelues, after the rule of the Sa-

I   cred

cred Word, to seeke his glory, with thofe *wayes*, that perish not. Therefore, this God, of his free grace, keepeth them in the right path; and by that direct courfe, conducteth them to the fame *bleffedneffe*, whereunto hee foreknew it would lead them. And, that this word, *knoweth*, may be vnderftood, as is aforefayd, to imply a *regard*, or *approbation*, appeareth in thefe enfuing places. *Pfal.* 101. 4. *Rom.* 8. 1. 5. 1. *Iohn* 3. 2. And fo much may be alfo prooued by that place of *Matthew*, where *Chrift* vfeth the contrary fpeech, to fhew the difrefpect that he would haue to the wicked. *I neuer knew you* (will he fay) *depart from me, yee workers of iniquity.* This word, *knoweth*, may haue refpect alfo to the fore-knowledge of their election. For (as fome vnderftand it) to that purpofe, S. *Paul* vfeth it in his fecond Epiftle to *Timothy*, chap. 2. and the 19. verfe. And writing

Iob 9. 12.
Prou. 12. 10.

Matth. 7. 23.

2 *Tim.* 2. 19.

the firſt Pſalme.

ting to the *Romans*, he ſaith. *Thoſe, whom he did forcknow, he did alſo predeſtinate, to be conformed to the Image of his Sonne.*   *Rom.* 8. 29.

But the way of the vngodly ſhall periſh. And that is; becauſe, God regardeth not, neither is delighted with their courſes. They propoſe vnto themſelues a happineſſe; but come ſhort of it: becauſe, their counſels, endeauours, and all; are ouerthrown, before they can attaine to the poſſeſſion therof. And needs muſt it be ſo. Seeing it is, neither the right means, which they vſe; nor, a true happineſſe, which they ſeeke. For, wherto tends their ayme? Sure, not to Gods glory; nor, to ſeeke their ſpirituall wel fare; nor any greater *bleſſedneſſe*, then the compaſſing, or enioying of ſome brutiſh, or tranſitory pleaſures. Which, before it be long, either altogether faile them; or, inſtead of a deſired happineſſe, are a

I 2   meanes,

meanes to bring vpon them the curse of some vnexpected miserie, which is euer the *period* of such *paths*. So, they at length, perceiue with much discomfort, that their labors are lost, their time mis-spent, & that (as the *Prophet* here saith) *Their way must perish*, and come to nought. In breefe then, I vnderstand these words, *The way of the vngodly shall perish*: As if the *Prophet* had sayd. The vngodly come short of blessednesse, and shall be excluded from the Congregation of the Iust; because, the Lord is regardlesse of them; and so, those vaine wayes and courses, which they follow, shall faile to bring them thither.

Obser. 1. Hence then, wee are taught, how to esteeme the world, with all those titles, honours, and fauours, wherewithall shee allureth us, to setle our hearts, vpon the painted and vncertaine felicities of this life: and to bee heed-

The first Psalme.

heedfull, that they draw vs not into the way of destruction. And, as the first part of the *Psalme*, ought to win vs, in respect of the felicitie, promised to *the way of the Righteous:* so, the ruine, that is heere threatned, may terrifie vs from *the way of sinners*.

Obser. 2.

Further, wee may hence learne, not to bee deiected, in our miseries, though wee are mercilesly oppressed, by our aduersaries; nor, be discomfited: because the world neither pities, nor takes notice, of those many slanders, and secret iniuries, which wee uniustly suffer. For, if God (as it is here sayd, hee doth) *knoweth*, and regardeth, *the way of his* seruants, wee may be certaine, that he seeth euery affliction in this iourney, and will not leaue our oppressions unreuenged.

Obser. 2.

We may also hence be taught; not to

to take offence at the fhort profperity of the wicked; nor, to bee allured with the pleafantneffe of their waies. For, though they bee delightfull to the fence, and goodly broad pathes; yet they lead to deftruction, and, as it is here told vs, they fhall perifh.

Thus, according to my abilitie, I haue gone thorow with an Expofition vpon this *Pfalme*. Wherein, though I haue followed no one; yet, I haue runne the ordinary way, with other Expofitors. But, becaufe I beleeue with S. *Auguftine*, there is no *Pfalme*, wherein the Author of it, had no refpect to *Chrift*. I will fhew you, how it may bee fo aptly applyed vnto him, as you fhall eafily beleeue; that, although it may be accommodated to all the Saints; yet, aboue others, the Bleffed Man (as we fay) *per Antonomafiam*, meanes *Chrift*; and, that this *Pfalme*, was principally intended of that *Iuft One*.

For,

the first Psalme.

For, it is a *Song*, or *Psalme*, wherin *blessednesse* is ascribed, to that thrice godly Man, who is no way guilty of any kinde of sinne; whether it be of transgression, omission, or originall. And who, but *He* only; (or those, who haue receiued it by *Him*) can be honoured with such innocency; or capable of so high a dignity, as this true *Blessednesse*: who alone, perfectly fufilled the Law? And was obedient, euen to the death? Doubtlesse, none. For, all that are so called, are so entitled by him. And hee, is that for-euer-blessed Man, whose foot *neuer walkt*, in the crooked *way of the vngodly*; nor, stood in the *slippery path of sinners*.

He it was, who in true humilitie, taught the simple truth; and neglecting the vain dignities of the world, neuer reposed himselfe, in the imperious *seat of the Scornfull*, whith the

I 4   disdain-

disdainfull *Pharisies*. He it is, whose delight is in fulfilling the Will and *Law* of his *Father*; and in the accomplishment therof, hee seriously exercised himselfe, both *day & night*. He, is that flourishing *Tree, planted by the pure riuers, of water of life; cleere as cryſtall, and proceeding from the Throne of God*: euen that Tree, which is planted in the middeſt of new *Ieruſalem*, and hath brought forth the fruit of our saluation, in *due ſeaſon*, and in the fulneſſe of time: according to the Scriptures.

This is he, *whoſe leafe ſhall not fall*. That is; his words ſhall not fall to the ground, but remaine euer flouriſhing, and serue to heale the *Nations*; according to the Prophecy of Saint *Iohn*. And doubtleſſe, *whatſoeuer he doth ſhall proſper*. But the wicked are not ſo: that is; the *Iewes* and other wicked perſecutors of *Chriſt*;

Reuel. 22.

Christ; with such as by Faith, put not on his righteousnesse; are in a quite contrary estate. Like *Chaffe scattered with the wind*; yea, in a miserable, vaine, and vnsetled condition. And therefore, when this our redeemer shall enter into *Iudgement* with the world; such an *Antipathie* will be betweene him, and vnrighteousnesse; as they shall not be able *to stand* before him. But, when the Children of his kingdome shall be congregated at his right hand, to partake with him in eternall blisse; as they haue beene partakers with him, in his graces here: then shall the wicked be shut out of their assemblies; to be cast into eternall perdition. And of this separation, the reason is; because the *Righteous* doe follow *Christ* in the *way* of his *Gospel*; and walke in the *Faith* which he hath approued. Whilst the *Iewes*, and

Exercises vpon

and such as are without the *Church:* seeking saluation by the workes of the *Law*, or following some such wrong, or by paths; their *way* failes them, and comes vnto an end, when it hath brought them to the left hand of the Iudge. Where; they are fartheft off from *Blessed-nesse.*

Medi-

the firſt Pſalme. | 123

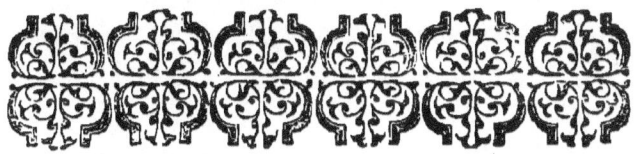

Meditations, vpon the firſt PSALME; in verſe.

The Contents of theſe Meditations.

The Muſe, firſt ſings the heauenly Bliſſe;
and ſhewes how vaine the earthly is.
The wrong way thither, with the right:
are here, laid open to your ſight.
The iuſt mans, glorious weal it ſhowes.
the ſinners, matchleſſe, endleſſe woes.
And good, and bad, are both expreſt;
that you may learne, and chuſe the beſt.

Y Ou; *whoſe ore-weary, reſtleſſe ſoules deſire;*
   The prime content, to which all creatures tend;
                                             And

Exercises vpon

And to that matchlesse Blessednesse *aspire*:
Which (though most seeke) most faile of in the end.
 Lo; here a heauenly Muse *points out the* way,
Wherein you safe may runne, and neuer more
In those blinde-crooked paths of danger stray;
Which haue misled so many heretofore.
 No prize *vnsought, or trifling newes she sings*;
But that, for which your many adventures are:
That, which to gaine; Rich, poore-men slaues & Kings,
doe howerly, watch and labour, sweat and warre.
 Yet most perhaps in vaine; For, what they get
By their endeauour in the Common Course
Yeeldes no felicities but Counterfeit:
And often, driues them on, from bad, to worse.
 Yong bloods, are snared with the painted sweetes
Of lust, or beauty: and beleeue that there,
Is full contentment. The rich glutton greetes
His boundlesse appetite, with curious fare.
 The worldling, makes inquest for happinesse;
And dreames, to finde it in a trade of gaine:
He in his Auarice himselfe doth blesse,
And as his thirst is, such his blisse doth faine.
 The happinesse of some, in rich attire,
High Titles, or vaine-glorious pompe depends;

A

The firſt Pſalme.

A louing wife, another doth deſire:
Good-toward Children, or vnfained friends.
 Kings, in their awfull thrones of Soueraignty ;
And vncontrould prerogatiues delight :
The Courtier, ſooths vp them in vanitie ;
And thinkes it heauen, to be their Fauourite.
 But they are all deceiu'd ; For, all theſe be
Vaine-fruitleſſe aymes ; like graſſe will beauty fade,
Luſt, will to loathing turne, and then ſhall he
Who there ſought happineſſe, be haples made.
 A hungry famine, may thoſe Creatures waſt
Which glut cram'd Epicures : or ſome diſeaſe,
May take away the pleaſure of the taſt.
And where is then, the happineſſe of theſe?
 Fire ; water, theeues or Ruſt, conſume the ſtore
Of richeſt men ; and he, that but to day
Had great poſſeſſions, is to morrow poore :
Or dies ; or ſees it, to his foes a pray.
 Gay cloathes, to Rags we haue exchanged ſeene.
Foule ſtinch, and wormes the proudeſt ruin'd haue.
And thoſe ; that dearer than their ſoules haue beene,
Haue ſhar'd their wealth, & laught thē to their graue
 She ; that hath kiſt, embrac't and ſworne to-day
A Thouſand vowes of kindeneſſe in thine arme:
           When

When thou art cold, and in a sheete of clay;
Shall keepe anothers bed and bosome warme.
 Those Princes, that have largest kingdomes got,
Are neuer quiet, whilst there doe remaine
Some other Emperies which they haue not:
Nay, if they might, the next, and next obtaine
 Till they had all. Perhaps they would be sad
(If not for some poore toy or Humor crost) *(had:*
That more things were not knowne which might be
Or lest, what they enioyed should be lost.
 What blisse affords a Crowne; when treasons, war,
And nightly cares, disturbes the owners rest?
More sad amid their armed troopes they are,
Then he that walkes alone with naked brest.
 Though all the meanes, to be secure they take
Some horror, still appeares their soules to grieue;
And greatnesse, neuer such a guard could make,
But sorrowes would get in, and aske no leaue.
 Though, they had all the pleasures of the sence,
And ten times doubled their prerogatiue;
Though Parasites *applaude their Excellence,*
And yeelde them adoration while they liue:
 Though they attained to as much, as he
Who on the Iewish *Throne next* Dauid *sate:*
         Had

the first Psalme.

Had so much wisedome, and could prying be
Through every Creature, to behold their state.
   When that were done; but little hope had they
From any thing on earth, content to gather.
That great wise Prince, made tryall; and could say:
That, to the soule they brought vexation rather.
   And, when pale death assailes; the thoughts & feare
Which trouble poorest men: shall ceaze their soule.
Their paines, shall be as sharpe as Bond mens are;
Their flesh shall stinke as much; and be as foule.
   Yea, er'e their breath forsake them one whole houre,
Their greatest glorie, may be turn'd to scorne;
But in one Age, the Rumor of their power
May be no more then his, that is vnborne.
   And then; alas! to what poore fortunes brought
Are those; whose blisse, on will of these, depends?
Such; as nor do, nor speake, nor scarce thinke ought;
But that, which to their Princes humor tends?
   For these; are Honours tennants but at will;
Which when he list, the giuer may recall:
And causelesse (if he please) obiect some ill;
To iustifie his dealing, with their fall.
   And what a miserable state were this,
For any, to be deemed happy in?
                                           Poore

*Poore soules awake; see; see what trust there is
In that, wherewith you haue deluded beene.*
  Let wantons, *seeke in lust what is not there.*
Let Epicures, *at Feasts for blisse enquire.*
Let Misers *looke on dust, till dust they are:*
And worldly men, *the worlds vaine loue desire.*
  Let Kings *of Earth; affect an earthly Crowne.*
Let Courtiers *at the Court attend their Fates.*
And whilst they catch the bubbles of renowne;
Let fooles; *still wonder, at their happy states.*
  But you; *that haue the end of these, descern'd,
And surer grounds of blessednesse would know:
Come, heare what of a* Prophet, *I haue learn'd:
Who, sung this heauenly subiect, long agoe.*
  He taught my Muse; *and you, she teacheth how,
Best beauties, best perfection to imbrace.*
With Angels foode, *she will replenish you;
And make you richer, then old* Adam *was.*
  In stead of mens false friendships, and their loue
Vnperfect, and inconstant, here below:
You, shall be deere vnto the Saints aboue,
And into fellowship with Angels grow.
  Where you shall loue, and be belou'd of all;
Without (the least) distrust, or Ielousie:
                                               And

the first Psalme.

And death, or time, of nought depriue you shall;
But yeeld content (at full) eternally.
  If, with your vanities, you can dispence,
And slight those fauors, which each worldling craues;
You shall be Fauorites, to that great Prince,
To whom, Earths greatest Monarks are but slaues.
  Such wished honours, She shall bring you to,
As Kings can neither giue; not take away.
And, that you may not feare, what flesh can do,
Shall be as free; and full as great as they.
  Yea, that true Blisse, to which all writings tend;
And most are yet to learne: here, know you shall.
By knowing, may enioy it in the end;
Enioying be contented there withall:
Vntill your soules, enriched with that store,
Shall neuer know desire, or lothing more.
  But, you must listen with attention then;
And hitherto, your vtmost power enforce:
For, 'tis not; 'tis not (oh you sonnes of men)
Obtain'd, by euery ordinary course.
  The way to blisse; is neither made by strength,
Nor humane policie. Though many a tract,
Makes shew of leading thither; yet, at length,
It turnes another way, and brings to wrack.

               K   The

The Pagans, *had a thought, some* God-head *should*
Direct them thither; and in feare they might,
Misse that good Deity, *which guide them could:*
They seru'd too many Gods, *and lost it quite.*

The old Philosophers (*not knowing this;*
That Nature, *by our fall, was growne corrupt*)
By Morall Vertues, *onely sought for blisse:*
Which did, their hoped Passage, interrupt.

For, when they had done all, which might be
By strict Morality, to gaine their passe; (*wrought,*
And time, their course, vnto an end had brought,
Their ayme they mist; because, Christ *wanting was.*

For, though some good they did; yet, missing him,
To sanctifie their vertues, and to take
Those faults away, which had escaped them:
Into this rest, no entrance could they make.

The blinded Iewes, *by ceremonious lawes,*
And strict obseruing of their ancient guise,
Haue labour'd for it; but, vpon some cause,
That way was long since chang'd, and from-ward lies

By vaine will-worship others goe. And some,
By formall shewes, of zealous sanctitie.
By way of their owne merits, many come:
And come farre short, of true felicitie.

A thou-

the firſt Pſalme.

A thouſand other, crooked paths there be;
Which ſeeme, to be direct; yet, lead aſtray:
Leſt therefore, ſome of thoſe, miſcarry thee,
That haſt a longing, to the bleſſed way;
  Who happy are; lo, here it ſhall be ſhowne,
  And how, thou mayſt thy ſelfe, be ſuch an one.

Vers. 1.

Bleſſed is the man, that doth not walke in the counſell of the vngodly, nor ſtand in the way of ſinners, nor ſit in the ſeat of the ſcornfull.

Firſt, get thee out of that vngodly way,
  (The way of Nature*) in which, all the race*
Of Adams *Progeny; haue gone aſtray.*
Walke out of it, into the way of Grace.
  To which, there lyeth no hard paſſage, thence:
For, if thou wade, but thorow Baptiſmes *ford*,
And paſſe the thorny hedge, of Penitence:
Thou ſtraight art guided thither, by the Word.

         Yet,

Yet, take thou heede, when thus thou entred art;
Lest that corruption, which doth still remaine:
By vaine affections, ill-aduise the heart,
To walke *with the* vngodly, *backe againe.*

  Cast not thine eyes about, on those gay bayts;
That grow, beside the way of Blessednesse:
But, shun thou all occasion, that awayts,
To draw thee into paths of wickednesse.

  Let not the loue of honour, pleasure, ease,
Reuenge, lust, enuy, pride, *or* auarice:
Nor any such ill Counsellours, *as these;*
Thy feet, vnto an euill course entice.

  Pursue not worldly things, as worldly men,
That know not God, or true religion, do:
But, giue his Honour first respect; and then,
With moderation, seeke the creature to.

  Let no desire, without that compasse stray;
Which honesty and piety hath set.
For, if thy thoughts doe euer breake away,
And Counsels *of vngodly longings get.*

  They will not leaue thee; but, from lust, to lust,
Allure thee on, in the vngodly path:
Vntill, they bring thee, to some act vniust.
And there, the sinners way *beginning hath.*

                                      Oh!

the first Psalme.

Oh! if through weaknesse, and attending to
Vngodly Counsels; *thou shalt thither rome:*
As all indeede (though all their best they doe)
Into the way, of euill doers, come.

  Yet, stand *not there; continue not in sin:*
But, by repentance, soone returne againe:
Lest, thou shouldst, by insisting long therin;
Affect it, and for euer there remaine.

  Vse, gets a habit; and the habit got,
The title of a Sinner, *gaineth thee:*
And sin, in this gradation resteth not,
Till to a Scorner, *thy Commencement bee.*

  And then beware. For, if degree thou take
So far; and be a Doctor of their Chaire:
The next progression, thou from thence canst make;
Is either hell immediate or dispaire.

  In thinking ill; we doe from heauen-ward goe;
In acting it, we further run astray:
But, if we to deride religion grow;
There's hardly hope, that we repent vs may.

  For, though God can the course of nature turne;
Bid aire descend, and earth aboue it rise:
Quench heat in fire, make frozen water burne;
And in all creatures, change the qualities.

Yet, that he therfore will; it followes not,
And so; although he can repentance giue,
To such, as haue a wicked habit got:
And, in despight of him and vertue liue.

   Assoone, shall I beleeue; that desperate Churle,
Who, from a rough steep cliffe, or high Tower wall,
Himself a furlong from the top doth hurle;
May raise himselfe, in middest of the fall:

   As that; the Sinner, *who, of wilfullnesse,*
Hath cast himselfe downe, from the hold of grace;
Can leaue that deep-deep gulf of wickednesse,
And in the rocke of mercy, get a place.

   It is a rare gain'd fauour, *when God daignes*
That vicious liuer grace, at his last breath:
Who, from no sinne, for loue of Good, refraines;
Nor, thinkes to aske forgiuenesse, vntill death.

   But, 'tis a Miracle, *if euer hee*
Shall, in his life, or death, forgiuenesse get;
Who knowes, and scornes, the means that profer'd be:
For, neuer was it found exampled yet.

   Of these three steps; oh! be yee wary then;
To sit, *or* stande, *or* walke, *doe you forbeare:*
In feat, *or* way, *or* counsell, *with those men;*
That Scorners, Sinners, *or* Vngodly *are.*

                                              Nor,

the first Psalme.

 Nor, will this be enough. For, as the Swaine,
Who sitteth downe, when he himselfe hath lost:
Is no more like, to reach his home againe;
Then he, that quite another way doth post.
 So they, who thinke it is enough, to shun
The ordinary path, that Sinners *tread;*
And take no heed, what good is to be done:
Shall neuer, of true happinesse be sped.
 Or, like as they; who, without Sterne or Card,
Dare seeke an vnknowne Coast, for golden ore:
May crowne their voyage, with a rich reward;
Assoone as those, that vse nor Saile, nor Oare.
 Right so; as well may such, as loosely liue,
The prize of happinesse attaine vnto:
As those; who hope, they shall at blisse ariue,
Although not one foot thither-ward, they goe.
 And therfore listen, my aduise vnto:
That you may learne, what you haue yet, to doe.

K 4   Vers.

Vers. 2.

But his delight is in the Law of the LORD, and in his Law doth he meditate day and night.

(hath;

WHen *Gods great mercy, safely brought thee*
From all the counsels, waies, *& feats of sin:*
Lest *thou stray backe againe;* take vp the path
That iust against it lies; *and walke therin.*
 Keepe on foreright; *let nothing tarry thee:*
For, non-progression, *there; regression is.*
But, *if thou in continuall motion bee;*
(Though slow it doth appeare) it brings to blisse.
 To helpe thee on, two sacred Scrowles *there are;*
Which may direct thy Pilgrimage *throughout:*
They profer'd are, to euery Passenger;
And can informe them, where they stand in doubt.
 The first sure marke, *that tels vs we are right,*
In this blest progresse, and haue quite abhord
The way of Sinners; is a true delight,
Vnto the Law, *of our* eternall LORD.

Whilst

The firſt Pſalme.

Whilſt that affection holds; there is no feare,
Or danger of relapſe. No wicked traine,
Which the vngodly roundeth in thine eare,
Can moue thee, to partake therein againe.

But, leſt thy heart deceiue thee (for mans heart
Is falſe, and oft betrayes him to his foe)
Make triall of his truth (if wiſe thou art)
And I will ſhew thee, how thou mayſt doe ſo.

Search, if there be no carnall vaine reſpect,
That drawes on this delight; or, if to thee
Thoſe volumes, which thou ſeemeſt to affect:
Be pleaſing, as the Word of God they bee.

Try, if thy Conſcience, will for witneſſe come,
That thou haſt, with a true endeauour, ſought
To exerciſe his Law; abroad, at home,
By day, by night, in deed, in word, in thought.

For, know well this, that by the Night and Day,
It is not onely meant, in weale and woe:
Or, that thou ſhouldſt, from time to time aſſay,
Vntired, in the way of Bliſſe to goe.

But, thou with knowledge, muſt proceed therin.
By pondering Gods Law, both in the Night,
Of his Old Teſtament, which veyl'd it in:
And in the New; that Day-like gaue it light.

Firſt,

First, thou must meditate, how man was made,
And (being made) a Law from God receiu'd:
How he transgrest, and fell; and falling, had
That Law (with some new circumstance) reuiu'd.

 Thou must consider, how the same was writ,
First, in the heart *by* nature; *then in* stone:
And how, in Essence, *neuer altring it.*
Of Accidents, *God added many a one.*

 Thou must conceiue; the prime Essentiall part
Of this great Law, *was* Christ: *and* Christ, *the End*
Of all those things, which thou inform'd of art;
Throughout the booke, *before his comming pend.*

 Thou must obserue, how euery passage there,
Doth shadow out that substance; and foretell,
In holy riddles, what did plaine appeare;
When his, so long-expected Day *befell.*

 Then, hauing passed o're the cloudy Night,
Of Types, *darke* Figures, *hidden* Prophesies,
And deepe Ænigma's; *thou must seeke the light,*
To be instructed in these Mysteries.

 Thou, in the Day, Gods Law *must meditate.*
The Day *of his* New Testament; *wherein,*
The Morning-Star *appear'd: and set a date,*
To that thicke darknesse, which so long had bin.

And,

the first Psalme.

 And, when thou seest how all the visions, dreams,
And Prophesies *obscure, discouered are;*
By those bright-shining, and thrice-glorious beames,
Which, at thy Saviours *comming did appeare.*
 Thou must (in that faire sun-shine of his grace)
Consider, with what infinite respect,
God daign'd to pity, thy distressed case:
And how much, Hee, thy well fare did affect.
 From poynt, to poynt, thou well consider must;
The Law *in his* New Testament *declar'd,*
The Law *of* Faith, *which makes the sinner iust:*
And opes the gate, which Adams *crime had barr'd.*
 Theron affix thy heart; and learne to know,
How God, from age to age, this Law *deriu'd.*
How, that of Moses, *did abolisht grow:*
With, what must be perform'd; and what beleeu'd.
 For, those who thus much learne; & teach, & then
Continue practise, in a course vpright:
May best enstiled be, those happy men;
That meditate Gods Law, both Day and Night.
 If this thou reach; or, but endeauor well,
To that degree of Grace, *which God shall daine:*
The Worthies *of the world, thou shalt excell;*
And win the prize, for which they seeke in vaine.
            Yea;

Yea; cheare thy foule; and let nor paine, nor care,
Nor loffe, nor height, nor depth, nor ought at all,
The world can tell thee; make thy foule to feare;
For this; to Bleffedneffe, *conduct thee fhall.*
 Nay, thou already, therein; bleffed art.
And euen, thofe ftormes of troubles, that oppreffe,
and hem thee round about, on euery part;
Shall make more perfect, thy true happineffe.
 Which will be fuch; as tongue-tide eloquence,
Shall be vnable to report thy bliffe :
Yea, fo vnthought of, is that excellence,
No heart, e're halfe imagin'd, what it is.
 And, ah! what pleafures can be more excelling;
 Then thofe, that are beyond both thought & telling?

Vers. 3.

And he, fhall be like a Tree planted by the riuers of waters, that will bring forth his fruit in feafon, his leafe fhall not fade, and whatfoeuer he doth, fhall profper.

But

the first Psalme.

BVt, sensuall men, must haue a sensuall touch,
Of what we tell them; and some obiects view:
By which, their reason, may perceiue as much,
As, either words, or signes, haue power to shew.
   For els, although the portion be but small,
Which they (at best) of these things can conceiue;
That little portion will be nought at all.
And (as in vaine) our labour we may leaue.
   That (therfore) you, some little glympse may see,
Of that abundance of contentment; which
Must wait on those, that this way happy bee:
And make them, without want, or loathing, rich.
   Marke well, those euer-green-leafe-bearing Trees;
Which, in some fruitfull valley planted are:
Where; with their nature, soyle, and clime agrees;
And riuers flow, to moyst them, all the yeare.
   Where, neither Summers heat, nor Winters cold,
Nor sterrile drought, nor rotting wet, offends.
But where, the aire doth such good temper hold,
That floures doe leaues, and fruits still floures attend.
   For, as those trees, may so much moysture take,
As they shall either neede, or can containe;
And nothing misse of, which compleat may make,
What to a trees well-being, doth pertaine.
                                          So;

 So, by the loue of Gods eternall law;
Mens soules, are set anew in Paradise.
Where; from the Riuers of Gods grace, they draw
The nourishments, of true felicities.
 Their state is constant, lasting euermore.
And not one true contentment, can be found,
In Earth, or heauens immesurable store;
But, with that wisht perfection they are Crown'd.
 Their soules haue all that full of happinesse,
Which can in any soule, contained be:
As trees, best planted; haue that fruitfulnesse,
Which most becomes the nature of a Tree.
 They in the Church, Gods Garden planted are;
Where Christ, that liuing rock, remaineth still.
And, from his side (the crimson Fountaine there)
Lifes pretious liquors, plentiously distill.
 His blessed Sacraments *and faithfull* Word,
Preserues their growth, and makes them fructifie;
Till they, doe fruit for euery Moneth afford,
And beare the leaues, of blest eternity.
 Neuer; no neuer, can their beauty fall
from ripe perfection; but, as you haue seene
A goodly bay-tree flourish: So, they shall
Be, winter, sommer, spring and Autumne greene.
And

the first Psalme. | 142

And then ; in all things, they shall prosper too ;
What er'e betide them ; or what ere they do.

Vers. 4.

The vngodly *are* not so : but
are like the chaffe which the
winde driueth away.

BVt, lest that all which hath been said should faile
To make you well conceiue, how much it may
Redound to euery seuerall mans auaile ;
To grow approued, in this blessed way.
 And since, the natures of most men, are such ;
As that, the promises of best contents,
Do seldome halfe preuaile with them so much,
As slauish feare, of threatned punishments.
 Know this ; that whatsoeuer mortall wight,
The way of life, here taught him, doth refuse :
He shall not onely, be depriued quite,
Of these ; and all those hopes, that he pursues.
 But, his condition, from the blessed, shall
So farre be differing ; that, no strife, vnrest,
         Shame,

Shame, horror, or misfortune, can befall:
But, his difpairing foule, it fhall arreft.
   If you e're noted haue, how far we prize
The lighteft chaffe, beneath the waighty graine;
How fafe the one is kept, how firme it lies;
How vile we count the other, and how vaine.
   Betwixt the worldling, and right-bleffed man;
Such difference is there. For, as euery winde,
The fleighted chaffe, doth this, and that way fan:
And no abiding place, will let it finde.
   So, that vngodly, irreligious crue,
Who make their heauen on earth; and fcorning thefe
True paths of bleffedneffe, thofe toyes purfue,
Which may their owne proud eye, or belly pleafe:
   Eu'n thofe; by puffes of windy vanity,
Strong-raging paffion, and vntamed luft:
Are hurried, with fuch ftrange incertainty,
To this, and that, euery act vniuft.
   As, whatfoeuer reft they feeme to take,
Their life is wholly reftleffe; and no day,
No houre, no minute, fleeping, or awake:
In any fetled peace, continue they.
   The Glutton would be rich; but is perplext,
To thinke, that he muft then abate his fare.

the first Psalme.

The Miser, *would haue honour*; *and is vext,*
To see how costly, courts and greatnesse are.
   Th' Ambitious, *couets ease*; *but findes it mars*
His high designes: *and may his hopes deface.*
The Coward, *would haue fame*; *but feares the wars*:
And Leachers, *doubt diseases, or disgrace.*
   Yea, in their hearts, so many strange desires,
Are often lodg'd, and those so opposite:
That, by enioying what one lust requires,
They bar themselues, some other wisht delight.
   But grant, their outward state were setled more,
More thriuing, and in losse, and changes lesse:
That they haue ease, and honour, with their store;
And to the world-ward, setled happinesse.
   Yet, neither can they wake, nor sleep in peace.
Their conscience, like a flaming-fire within;
Will seare, and scorch, and burne: *and neuer cease*
Vntill dispaire, *to nestle there begin.*
   Or say they scape this to. *And whilst they liue,*
So stupid grow, that in securitie,
They senselesse lie; *vntill their soules, it driue*
Into a helplesse, hellish lethargie.
   Yet, which is worse; *far worse, then what is past*:
(And makes me tremble, when I call to minde

L

Their

Their fearfull cause) there is a Day *at last;*
In which they pay for all, that is behinde.
   But, those sad terrours will my Muse *rehearse,*
In what she singeth, on the following Verse.

VERS. 5.

Therefore the Vngodly shall not stand in the Iudgement, nor Sinners in the Congregation of the Righteous.

O*H you! whom neither Gods eternall loue,*
  Nor vertues beauty, nor his sacred Law;
Nor promises of matchlesse Blisse, *can moue:*
Nor threatned losse therof, preserue in awe.
  You; that are neither wooed to repent,
Your follies, for this lifes vncertainties:
Nor won, to seeke the way of true content;
By inward feares, nor outward miseries.
  Though none of these, can gaine you to assay,
For that high Blessednesse, *which crownes the good;*
                                                    Nor,

the firſt Pſalme.

Nor force you, to forgoe that damned way,
Which ſeemeth pleaſing, vnto fleſh and blood.
  Oh yet! for that rare priuiledge, which thoſe,
Who loue Gods Law, ſhall haue; when flaming fire,
Doth all this maſſie Globe of earth encloſe:
To rectifie your courſe, I you require.
  For know; there are not onely, in this world,
A thouſand miſcheefes, plagues, heart-ſtinging cares,
And dreadfull Iudgements; ready to be hurld,
From Heauens high Battlements, about your eares:
  But, after death, there is a time will come,
To haſten all, which is delayed here.
A Day of vengeance, and a Day of Doome:
In which; all Adams Of-ſpring, ſhall appeare.
  The dreadfull Iudge, in glory will deſcend;
With his great Hoſt of Heauen, compaſt round.
Seas, Earth, and Hell, ſhall at his Bar attend,
With al their priſoners, when the Trump doth ſound.
  A hideous Bonefire, through the world ſhall blaze.
The Roofe of Heauen, ſhall like a parchment ſcrowle,
At his appearing, ſhrinke; and with amaze,
The dead ſhall riſe; the liuing, frighted howle.
  And, neither ſex, condition, nor degree;
Shall haue reſpect, or place: but every one,

L 2 Without

Without diſtinction, ſhall in perſon bee;
Before the great Almighties *Iudgement Throne.*
　Your pureſt beauties, ſhall attract no more,
That Iudges *eye; then fouleſt vlcers can.*
He, *ſhall not bribed be, with* Indian *Ore:*
Nor moued, by the flattring tongue of man.
　Kings, *are in his eſteeme no more that* Day,
Then ſlaues: or, pooreſt wretches on the earth.
He, *prizeth no man, for his rich aray:*
Nor ought regardeth, nobleneſſe of birth.
　In his Grand Court *of Iuſtice; he admits,*
No ſubtill Trauers, *no* Demurs, Repeales,
Delayes, Iniunctions, *neither any* Writs
Of Error, *nor* Excuſes, *nor* Appeales.
　No bribed Fauorites, *hath* Hee *to raiſe,*
By motions at his Bar: *On him, attends*　　(*ſwayes:*
No Groomes, *nor* Kinſmen, *that his* Lordſhip
To wreſt the courſe of Iuſtice, to their ends.
　No great man *ſends his letters to entreat,*
To change his ſentence; nor a coſtly fee:
That hires him any way to mitigate,
What he hath once, reſolued to decree.
　You ſons of Adam; *you ſhall doubtleſſe come,*
(*Though ſleight perhaps my counſell may appeare.*
　　　　　　　　　　　　　　　　　　　To

the first Psalme.

To such a Iudge; to such impartiall Doome:
And finde all true, that I foretell you here.
   Yea; if you hearken not to the command
Of your Creator; nor, his Law delight:
You shall not in that Iudgement guiltlesse stand.
But fall condemned, in the Iudges sight.
   And, when the Righteous, are assembled there:
With, Come you Blessed. And at full possesse,
(According to the promise, made them here)
The ioyfull Crowne of endlesse happinesse.
   Then, with a curse excluded, shall you goe;
Amongst the damned spirits, into hell:
Shut out from blisse, into a world of woe;
Amid those tortures, which no tongue can tell.
   And when, as many hundred thousand yeares,
You haue endur'd; as there be on the shore,
Small stones, or sands: the time no shorter weares;
Nor will your plagues grow fewer, then before.
   Nay, though you were reseru'd for no more paine,
Nor other discontentment, then the misse,
Of that great good, to which the iust attaine:
In (such priuation) hell enough there is.
   We see, that when ambitious men haue got
Respect, and meanes enough, to liue at rest:

L 3   Yet,

Yet, if they miſſe ſome marke, wherat they ſhot;
They fret, as men without compare vnbleſt.
  We ſee that Worldlings; *who, on tempting gold,*
Haue ſet their thoughts, can ten times better beare
The brunt of labour; hunger, thirſt and cold:
Then liue well fed, and warme; with coffers bare.
  We likewiſe know; that Louers, *barr'd the ſight*
Of their deare Miſtreſſes; *can ne're receiue*
Content; nor cauſe of comfort, or delight:
Though free from outward paines, or want, they liue.
  Nay rather; it torments, and greeueth more
Their vexed ſoules, then ſmart of body may:
And more, themſelues, they thinke inſulted ore;
Then if, for triall, on the Racke they lay.
  This we haue knowne. And if, priuation can
On earth ſo torture; where euen torments are
Imperfect. Oh! how much more greeuous than,
Shall thoſe ſoules finde it, that muſt feele it there?
  If here; thou canſt not brooke contempt, diſgrace;
To be depriu'd of honour, or the view
Of thoſe falſe beauties; wherein thou do'ſt place
Contentment here. Ah! what will there enſue?
  How? how, wilt thou endure it, wretched Elfe?
When thou ſhalt know, what riches they poſſeſſe,
                                                     Who

the first Psalme.

Who shall be blessed: and perceiue thy selfe
Debarr'd, for euer, of that happinesse?
   When thou eternally, shalt be a scorne;
Of thy contentment stript; of peace, of friends:
Of all the fellowship of Saints, forlorne;
And no Companions left, but damned Fiends.
   When thou; to endlesse darknesse banished,
Shalt burne with the desire, of seeing Him.
With whose perfections, Angels eyes are fed;
And in respect of whom, the Sun is dim?
   Oh! what a passion will torment thy soule;
When thou shalt misse that sweetnesse? And imbrace,
Insteed therof; deformity, as foule,
As hell, can put vpon her lothsome face.
   What wilt thou doe, alas! when thou must beare
All this great horror; and sharp pangs withall?
For thus; euen thus, will the vngodly fare:
When that great Iudgement, ouertake them shall.
   And it shall adde, vnto their torment to;
   What e're they suffer, say, or thinke, or do.

VERS. 6.

For, the LORD knoweth the way of the Righteous: but the way of the Vngodly ſhall periſh.

Vt that no righteous *Man, deterr'd may be,*
From labouring, for his Bleſſedneſſe, *through*
That the Almighty, *doth nor mark, nor ſee: (doubt,*
How many painfull ſteps, he paceth out.
 And likewiſe, that no Sinner *may, vnwarned,*
His owne vaine way purſue, with falſe ſurmize:
That God doth ouer-paſſe, as vndiſcerned;
The courſe he takes; or winke at villanies.
 Know this, you happy men, that would attaine
To perfect Bliſſe. *That, howſoe're you ſeeme*
Obſcur'd on earth; and oft to ſpend in vaine,
Your labours, and your liues, without eſteeme.
 There's not a drop of bloud, a ſigh, a teare,
An inward ſmarting, or an outward grone.

the first Psalme.

A sleight vnkindnesse, or a scoffe you beare:
But the Almighty knowes them, every one.
  If you but sweat a little, in this path:
He sees it; and in time, reward it will.
Not one sad thought, your heart in secret hath:
But God both knowes therof, and mindes it still.
  Though you close prisoners were, in strictest thrall,
Neglected of the world, and seene by none,
But such oppressours, as would smother all,
Which for your praise, or comfort, might bee knowne.
  Though you were mew'd, where none might come to (tell,
What you haue done, or suffer'd, in this way:
And being in some dungeon, forc'd to dwell;
Had mourn'd, to death, shut from the sight of day.
  Yea, though your foes should labour, to obscure
Your good endeavours, with a slanderous fame;
And brand you, with vile actions so impure,
That all men thought you, worthy death and shame.
  Yet, God; whose bright, and all beholding eyes,
Viewes present, past, and euery future thing:
Sees vndeceiu'd; and whatsoe're he spies,
To light, will one day, to your glory bring.
He knowes; & knowing, doth approue your course.
And what he doth approue, shall neuer faile.
                                             Nor

Nor Man, nor Deuill; policie, nor force:
Against his power, or knowledge, can preuaile.
 Oh therfore! droop not, though a thousand stormes,
Or likelyhoods of ruine, may appeare:
For, when dispaire puts on her vgliest forme;
Then; is your most assured safety neere.
 Nor boast, you Sinners; as if you had found
A readier course, vnto the truest blisse,
Then righteous men; because, your way is crown'd
With more vaine honour, then their labour is.
 Nor, let your painted pleasures, gull you so;
To make you dreame, that God deceiu'd will bee.
Or, that an vnsuspected course you go:
Because, the world your danger cannot see.
 For, though a while you prosper, and delude
With shewes of happinesse, the blinded eye
Of fooles; and the abused multitude,
That are in loue, with your gay vanity.
 Yet; ruine, shame, and desolation shall
Confound your way. And vpon euery one,
That therein walketh, will destruction fall.
Euen then; when least (perhaps) you thinke theron.
 Though, in the world; you long haue had the names
Of honourable, honest, iust, and wise:
Walkt

the first Psalme.

Walkt in a course approu'd, and left your fames
To after ages; in large Histories.
   Though you are great; and Orators can hire;
To cloke your foule proceedings, with faire showes;
Or, to defame the Righteous, here conspire.
And make abhorr'd, the path in which he goes.
   Though, at your deaths, with formall pietie,
And workes of publike loue, you often do
Conceale, your rotten hearts hypocrisie:
Deceiuing so, your selues, and others to.
   And, at your funerals, haue preacht abroad;
A glorious rumor, of a blessed end:
Those clouds, can neuer blinde the sight of God.
But ruine, shall your wicked course, attend.
   Though you; the ancient Heathens *prais'd mora-*
The Iewish *strictnesse*; the hot Zealousnesse   (*lities*;
Of Schismaticks *haue learn'd:* with Romes *forma-*
To trim your way, with shewes of happinesse. (*lities,*
   And though, the Passenger *that walks it, carries*
A lode of pardons: mumbling, as he goes,
Fiue thousand Creedes; ten thousand Aue Maries:
And, of his owne good merits, addes to those.
   Yet, all will faile him; yea, there's many a one,
By you, for Saints canoniz'd; whom your path
                                            Hath

Hath thither brought: where, now they lie & grone,
Beneath the burthen of Gods heauy wrath.
   For, he, approues no meanes of *happinesse*,
Or way of seruing him; but that which he
Hath taught himselfe: And, it is *wickednesse*;
Another course to seeke, what e're it be.
   This you haue done, you sinners; so, for this:
Your way, and you, shall perish. And while those
Whose course you haue derided; dwell in blisse;
You; all contentment, shall for euer lose.
   That (since you would not vnderstand aright,
The path *that leads to safety*; *whilst you might*)
You should, *when you are past returning*; know,
It was the Way, *that you despised so*.

* * * * * * * *

THus; haue I sung the sum, of what the *Muse*
Of our great *Prophet*; in this *Ode*, pursues.
The way to *Blisse*. Which, as my weakenesse can,
I striue to leuell so; that euery man;
Yea, little children, may come walke along:
And make it short, and easie, with a *song*.
                                         Here,

the first Psalme.

Here, warne I all; but here, I cannot say
Enough, to perfect all men, in that *way*.
For, some lacke one thing; some another misse,
To further on, their voiage vnto *blisse*. (ledge want.
Some, faith; some, works; some, loue; some know-
In some, repentance; in some, grace, is scant.
The greatest part; defectiue finde, I shall,
Of most of these; and many men of all.
Then, some dispaire; and some presume as far.
Some, too secure; and some, too pensiue are.
Some, pray not; and some, praise not God aright.
That each man therfore; he, well furnish might,
For this aduenture; and with meanes diuine,
Assist him, from his heauenly *Magazine*.
To fit their seuerall wants; he offers you
A hundred nine and forty (in a row)
Of such Instructions: as, who e're shall please,
To weigh their vse, and liue, and walke, by these.
My life for theirs; at length, they shall attaine
That happinesse, their soules, desires to gaine.
And to assist their weake simplicities,
That cannot sute, their owne necessities,
In that rich treasurye. My humble *Muse*
Shall be their Guide; their Seruant; and refuse

No

No paines (if Gods great Prouidence permit)
Till all thefe facred *Oracles*, fhe fit
To their capacities. So, I fhall be
A help to them: And they may further me,
By their good prayers, in that bleffed path:
Whofe end, contentment, euerlafting hath.

THE

the firſt Pſalme.

THE
PARAPHRASE;
WHERIN THE WORDS
of the Pſalme, are wholy retained : and diſtinguiſhed from *the reſt by a change of* LETTER.

B*leſſed is the man, that,* being in the firſt eſtate of innocency *doth not walke* from it, after the euill affections of corrupted nature : *in the* lewd *Counſels of the vngodlie*; By conſenting vnto euill concupiſcences, *Nor ſtand in the* broad *way of ſinners*, acting, and perſeuering in euill : *Nor ſit, in the* infectious *ſeat of the ſcornfull*; ſcoffing vertue, deriding religion ; or, by falſe doctrines
(and

Verſe 1.

(and euill examples) peruerting o-
thers.

Verſe 2. For, hee is ſuch an one; who, is
not carefull onely, to auoyd euill.
But, is enclined to good alſo. *His delight is* ſeriouſly *in the Law of the*
Lord. *And, in his* eternall *Law*
(that hee may know, teach, and fulfill it; in thought, word, and deed)
doth he meditate vpon all occaſions;
and at all times; euen, *Day and night*,
without intermiſſion.

Verſe 3. In this; conſiſteth the meanes of
his felicity. *And he ſhall be like a* flouriſhing *Tree*; which, the Diuine Prouidence hath *planted, by the riuers of
waters*. For, as ſuch a Tree, being
nouriſhed by thoſe ſtreames, hath
the meanes *that will* enable *it*, to *bring
forth his fruit in due ſeaſon*: ſo, the
Bleſſed Man, being planted by the
fountaines of Grace, flowing from
the Holy Spirit of God; bringeth
forth in due time, the fruits of faith,
and

and good workes, to eternall life. And, in the greateft drought, receiueth fuch refrefhing; that *his leafe fhall not fade.* A word of his, fhall not be in vaine (though, for the prefent, it feeme to fall to the ground) but it fhall take effect. *And whatfoeuer he doth fhall profper,* at laft; both to his euerlafting glory and the inftruction of others.

Now, *the vngodly*; becaufe, they walke after their owne Counfels, *are not fo* bleffed: neither, doth any thing they take in hand, fo profper. *But,* they, *are like the chaffe, which the winde driueth away.* For, as that is dry, vnfruitfull, and therfore carried about with euery puffe; fo, they wanting the moyfture of grace, are therfore ouer-light; and the fpirit of the Deuill, the winde of pride, temptations, and euill affections: vnfetledly hurrie them to and fro, without reft.

Verfe 4.

M   And,

Verſe 5.	And, by reaſon of this; euen be-cauſe, theſe vanities carry them from God. *Therfore, the vngodly ſhall not* be able to *ſtand,* as innocent, before him, *in the Iudgement.* Whether it be that, which he ſhall be pleaſed to inflict on them, in this life: or, at the laſt Day. *Nor,* ſhall falſe worſhip-pers, or ſuch *Sinners*; who haue neg-lected this meanes of Bleſſedneſſe: be admitted *in the Congregation of the Righteous,* among thoſe, to whom God (hauing ſeparated them at his right hand) ſhall hereafter ſay: Come, yee bleſſed of my Father, &c.
Verſe 6.	And all this, commeth thus to paſſe. *For* that, *the* LORD accep-teth, *knoweth,* and alloweth, *the* vn-defiled *way of the Righteous,* and the courſes, which they follow, to attaine this bleſſedneſſe. *But*, contrariwiſe, ſo abhorreth *the way of the vngodly*; that the endeauors, of thoſe Repro-bates,

the firſt Pſalme.

bates, *ſhall periſh*, with them, in eternall damnation.

The Prayer:

Wherin, the ſcope of this Pſalme is conſidered: and the bleſſedneſſe there mentioned, implored of God.

OH thou eternall Son, of the euer-liuing God. Who, art the way of life, the meanes of all true *Bleſſedneſſe*, and the onely Happy One; who, continuing in thy integrity, haſt both auoyded, all manner of ſinne; and euery way fulfilled the whole Law, and will of thy Father. Thou, oh Chriſt; who art that *tree of life*, which brought forth the fruit of our ſaluation, in *due ſeaſon*: and without whom, none can euer haue sure hope, to become happy. Grant, oh sweet Redeemer; that by the imputation of thy righteousnesse; we, who are fallen from our first Integrity, may bee regenerated, and made spotlesse againe, in thy sight. Sanctifie our polluted hearts, that they may no more wander after, the vaine *counsels*, of *vngodly* affections. Let them not haue power, to allure vs into the *way* of sinfull actions. Or, if we doe (through frailty) at any time, stray from Thee, into the trodden path of *Sinners*, which leadeth to destruction (as wee must acknowledge, we often doe.) Bring vs backe, oh sweet *Iesu*; and let vs not *stand* there, vntill we lose the feeling of our sinnes: and forget for euer to returne; but, let euery slip be attended, with immediate repentance, to whip vs vp againe; lest the iteration of sinne, bring vs at length, to the *seat of scorners*, and the deniall of

the firſt Pſalme.

of Thee. Keepe vs; oh keepe vs, from that low ebb of grace; yea, although we often run far into the *way of ſinners*; and many times careleſly *ſtand* ſtill, when thou calleſt vs from thence: yet, of all mercies, wee entreat thee, that we neuer bee ſuffered to ſtray ſo wide, from the way of *Bleſſedneſſe*: to ſin againſt thy Holy Spirit. Or, to *ſit* downe in that *ſeat* of *peſtilence*, which may infect our ſoules, to eternall death.

And, to enable vs the better, to ſhun ſuch dangers; we beſeech thee, poſſeſſe our hearts with thy loue; and a true delight in thy Word. Let thy *Law, day and night*, openly and ſecretly, in aduerſity and proſperity, bee our principall ſtudy, and practiſe, all the time of our life. Faſhion vs, to thine own Image; let thy right hand *plant* vs, in thine owne Vineyard.

And, that we may bee, as fruitfull-flouriſhing *Trees*, bringing forth ſeaſonable

M 3

fonable fruits, to thy glory, and the profit of thy *Church*. Let the plentifull *Riuers* of thy Grace, water vs; vntill we grow vp, and become fit to bee replanted, in thy eternall *Paradife*. Let our words, as the *leaues* of a fruitfull tree; be a continuall ornament vnto vs: feruing alfo, to heale the wounded confciences of our weake brethren. And although, for a time, thou fuffereft vs, to appeare miferable and vnhappy; yet, let all things (euen the afflictions which we haue had) *profper* vs in the way, to euerlafting *Bleffedneffe*.

And, forafmuch, as thofe, who delight not in thy feruice, are in a miferable condition; and nothing fo happy, as thy children, whatfoeuer they feem to the world. Grant, ô Lord, that wee (being warned by thy difpleafure againft them) may truly worfhip thee, & haue euer fuch a meafure of faith, and of thy grace; as may keep vs

the firſt Pſalme.

vs fetled in our confciences, & quiet, from the fury of thofe affections, that carry them headlong into endleffe vnreſt. And when thou fhalt caſt that *chaffe*, into the fire; purge vs, thy feruants, from corruption; and lay vs up, as pure wheat, in thy Heauenly Granard.

Heare vs, oh deere Redeemer; and when that dreadfull day commeth, wherein thou fhalt fummon the whole world to *Iudgement*. Let vs not, be thruſt among thofe guilty ones, who fhall fall, and bee confounded with horrour, at thy prefence. But make vs able to *ſtand*, in that fearfull doome; place vs at thy right hand, in that righteous Congregation, into which, no vnrepentant *ſinners* fhall be admitted. And, when thou fhalt turne them off, with that terrible anfwer; *I know you not.* Let vs; oh let vs, bee receiued into thy mercy. And feeing, wee feeke for

Bleſſed-

Blessednesse, by that way and meanes onely, which thou haſt appoynted: Acknowledge it, as thine owne ordinance; and, though we are a while the ſcorne of the world, make vs at length, Inheritors of that vnſpeakable felicity, which wee ſhall enioy in Thee. So, both in our ſafeties, and in the deſtruction of thine enemies alſo; ſhall thy name be glorified, now and for euer. *Amen.*

(***)

To

the firſt Pſalme. | 169

To fill vp the vacant pages of this ſheet, here is added, as neceſſary, to ſtir the Reader vp to theſe ſtudies; a metricall Paraphraſe, vpon the firſt eight verſes, of the 12 Chapter of *Eccleſiaſtes*, beginning thus:

Remember thy Creatour, in the dayes of thy youth, &c.

NOw Young-man; *thy Creator thinke vpon*;
   Before the prime, of luſty Youth *be gone.*
Now; *e're at hand, that euill day appeares*;
With thoſe vnwelcome and abhorred yeares:
When thou (deiected) ſhalt, the world contemne,
And grieued ſay; I haue no ioy in them. *(retaine,*
   Now; *whilſt* Sun, Moone, *and* Stars, *their light*
And no black clouds, *doe threat a ſecond* raine.
Before, the Keepers of the houſe *doe ſhrinke.*
Before, with trembling knees, the Strong men *ſinke.*
Before, the Grinders *leſs'ned, quiet lye*;   *prye.*
And they *grow* darke, *that through the* windowes
                                            Before

Before, the Doores without, *faſt cloſed bin,*
Through their baſe ſound, that faintly grinde *within.*
Before, the Bird *to riſe, doth ſummon thee* ;
And Muſiques Daughters *quite abaſed bee.*
Before, the lofty thing *doe this diſmay* ;
And ſhuddring feare *ſurprize thee in the* way.
Before the Almond *put his flowers abrode,*
The Graſhopper, *become a heauy lode,*
Deſires *decay, and lothed* Age *thou meet* ;
Or troops of Mourners, *waiting in the ſtreet.*
    Oh, doe not thou the time, till then prolong.
But minde him, whilſt the ſiluer Cord *is ſtrong.*
Now ; *whilſt the* Golden Ewre, *vncras'd is found :*
And at the Fountaine-head *the* Pitcher *found.*
Before the Wheele, *be at the* Cyſterne *tore,*
Or Duſt *grow earth, as earth it was before :*
And, from the bodies quite diſſolued frame ;
The ſoule returne to God, from whence it came.
    Thus ſpake the Preacher. And he told vs why :
    For all (ſayd he) is vaineſt vanity.

The

the first Psalme.

The same, another way paraphrased, according to the signification of the feuerall Metaphors.

(heat,
NOw ; whilst warme bloud, with fresh & kindly
Doth through each part, with liuely vigor beat:
And all thy beauties, in their spring-tide bee ;
Thinke on thy God, that so created thee.
Accept this fit aduantage of the time.
Giue him, the First-lings of thy golden prime.
Before, thy last vnwelcome dayes, begin
To bring those yeeres, thou hast no pleasure in.
Now ; while thou seest prosperities bright Sun,
Enlightens thee the way thou hast to run :
And Gods pure Word *affords a cheerfull light,*
To guide thee safely, through blacke errors night.
  Doe not forget, that thou a Maker *hast,*
Till all the morning of thy life be past.
Nor waste the time (from stormes & troubles cleare)
Till greefes on greefes ; like clouds on clouds appeare.
  Those hands, *that youth a while doth powerfull*
Vnsteddy (through their feeblenes) shall shake. (make;
                                             Those

Thofe legs, *that ftrongly doe vphold thee, now;*
With aches pained, fhall beneath thee bow.
Thy few loofe teeth, *will ceafe their food to grinde;*
And thy dim eyes, *ftand in their cazements blinde.*
Thy iawes, *their nimble motion quite fhall lofe.*
Thy lips *funke in, their double wickers clofe.*
Thy wonted fleepe, *thy temples fhall forgoe;*
And daily raife thee, when the Cocke *doth crow.*
Thy liftning eares, *their fenfe afide fhall lay:*
And euery rub, *difturb thee in the way.*
The filuer haires, *thou on thy head fhalt haue:*
Will fhew thee ready ripened for the graue.
Each trifling thing, *fhall be a burthen to thee.*
The vaine defires *of youth, fhall all forgoe thee.*
Thee; to his houfe, fhall Age *with panting breath*
Conduct; there lodge thee, in the bed of death,
And thofe, who thither, thy attendants were,
Shall mourning, *home returne; and leaue thee there.*

   Oh thou! that wouldft a needfull comfort finde,
In thofe blacke dayes; now thy Creator *minde.*
Before thy nerues *their finewie vigor lacke:*
And ftrength, and marrow, *leaue thy weakned back,*
While neither cares, *nor forrowes, craze thy* braine:
Whilft thy found liuer, *fills vp every vaine.*

                                         Whilft

the firſt Pſalme. | 173

Whilſt thou art yet in health ; *and feel'ſt thy* head,
By no heart-breaking pang diſtempered.
Ere fleſh *diſſolue to earth* ; *and* ſpirit *bee*
Return'd to Him, *that firſt did giue it thee.*
For then ; *this ſaying will moſt true appeare :*
That all is vaine, and nought but vaineſſe here.

Glory be to God.   Amen.

Correct these faults with thy pen.

Pag. 8. lin. 15. for *seemes*, read *seeme.* pag. 14. lin. 7. for *Catalicticall,* in some coppies, read *Cabalisticall.* pag. 119. lin. the last, for *whith,* read *with.* pag. 121. lin. 9. for *Righteousnesse,* in some coppies, read *Vnrighteousnesse,* pag. 124. lin. 23. for *thirst,* read *thrift.*

The Authours *Preparation to the Psalter,* somtime mentioned in this Booke, is to bee sold at the signe of the golden Vnicorne, in *Pater Noster* Row, by *Iohn Harrison.*

www.ingramcontent.com/pod-product-compliance
Lightning Source LLC
Chambersburg PA
CBHW032145160426
43197CB00008B/782